Albert Stanburough Cook

The Bible and English Prose Style

Selections and Comments

Albert Stanburough Cook

The Bible and English Prose Style
Selections and Comments

ISBN/EAN: 9783744692885

Printed in Europe, USA, Canada, Australia, Japan

Cover: Foto ©Thomas Meinert / pixelio.de

More available books at **www.hansebooks.com**

THE BIBLE AND ENGLISH PROSE STYLE

Selections and Comments

EDITED WITH AN INTRODUCTION

BY

ALBERT S. COOK

PROFESSOR OF THE ENGLISH LANGUAGE AND LITERATURE
IN YALE UNIVERSITY

BOSTON, U.S.A.
PUBLISHED BY D. C. HEATH & CO.
1892

Entered, according to Act of Congress, in the year 1892, by
ALBERT S. COOK,
in the Office of the Librarian of Congress, at Washington.

ALL RIGHTS RESERVED.

TYPOGRAPHY BY J. S. CUSHING & CO., BOSTON, U.S.A.
PRESSWORK BY BERWICK & SMITH, BOSTON, U.S.A.

TO

MY FRIENDS

AND SOMETIME FELLOW-WORKERS

THE ENGLISH TEACHERS OF CALIFORNIA

CONTENTS.

	PAGE
INTRODUCTION.	ix
ILLUSTRATIVE COMMENTS.	xxvii
Importance of the Bible to the Student of English.	xxvii
English Imitators of Biblical Language	xxxv
The King James Version.	xxxvii
Rhetorical Features of Biblical Language	xliii
Rhythm of the Bible	l
Biblical Style and Language Contrasted with those of Western Nations.	lix
BIBLICAL SELECTIONS.	1
Exodus 15	1
Exodus 20	3
Deuteronomy 32	5
2 Samuel 1. 17–27	9
1 Kings 8	10
Psalm 23	16
Psalm 32	16
Psalm 90	17
Psalm 91	18
Psalm 103	19
Psalm 112	21
Psalm 119	21
Psalm 139	32
Proverbs 2	33

BIBLICAL SELECTIONS — *Continued.*

	PAGE
Proverbs 3	34
Proverbs 8	36
Proverbs 12	39
Isaiah 58	40
Matthew 5	42
Matthew 6	45
Matthew 7	48
The Acts 26	50
1 Corinthians 13	52
1 Corinthians 15	53
James 4	57
Revelation 5	58
Revelation 6	60

THE BIBLE AND ENGLISH PROSE STYLE

INTRODUCTION.

TO enrich and ennoble the language of a race is to enrich and ennoble the sentiments of every man who has the command of that language. This process of enrichment and ennoblement has been going on in English for nearly thirteen hundred years, and one of the chief agencies by which it has been effected is the influence, direct and indirect, of the Bible. The first coherent words of English speech which have been transmitted to us are in a species of verse which suggests, though somewhat remotely, the rhythms and parallelisms of Hebrew poetry; they constitute a hymn of praise [1]

[1] I subjoin this most ancient specimen of English:

> Nu scylun hergan hefaenricaes uard,
> metudæs maecti end his modgidanc,
> uerc uuldurfadur; sue he uundra gihuaes,
> eci dryctin, or astelidæ.
> He aerist scop aelda barnum
> heben til hrofe, haleg scepen.
> Tha middungeard, moncynnæs uard,
> eci dryctin, æfter tiadæ,
> firum foldu, frea allmectig.

Which may be literally translated (case-signs in Italics):

> Now [we] shall glorify heaven-kingdom's Warden,
> Creator's might and his mood-thought [*sc.* counsel]
> Work [*or,* works] *of the* Glory-father; as he *of* wonders *of* each [*sc.* of each of wonders, of every wonder],
> Eternal Lord, [the] beginning established.
> He erst shaped *of* men *for the* children [*sc.* for the children of men]
> Heaven to [*sc.* for] roof, holy Shaper [*sc.* Creator].
> Then Midgard [*sc.* the earth], mankind's Warden,
> Eternal Lord, after prepared,
> For men [the] earth, Lord almighty.

which includes a paraphrastic rendering of the first verse of Genesis, and whose diction throughout is colored by Scriptural reminiscences. A single word will suffice to illustrate the statement last made. This word is contained in the first line of Cædmon's Hymn, and in its ancient spelling appears as *hefaenricaes*. What is the meaning of *hefaenricaes*? In modern English it would appear as *heavenric's*, the possessive of *heavenric*, a word which would be akin in formation to *bishopric*. The first element of the compound is easily distinguished; the second (identical with the German *Reich*) means *kingdom*. Hence the expression as a whole is (except for the final *s*, the sign of the genitive) the equivalent of the phrase so common in Matthew's Gospel, but found nowhere else in the Scriptures, *the kingdom of heaven*, or, more literally, *of the heavens*. With this New Testament phrase may be contrasted another which owes its origin to the Old Testament. Such an one occurs in the fifth line of the Hymn, as *aelda barnum*, signifying *for the children of men*. From no other conceivable source could this idiom have been derived except from the Scriptures of the Old Testament. It occurs several times in the Psalms, as well as sporadically in Genesis, Proverbs, and other books. That it should have originated among the English themselves is highly improbable, and there is no other language in which it is known to occur save as a translation or adaptation from the Hebrew. The conclusion already propounded is therefore the only one which it is possible to admit.

From Cædmon's time to the present the influence of Bible diction upon English speech has been virtually uninterrupted. The Latin of Bede, like that of all the later Fathers of the Church, is saturated with its peculiarities. To them the Vulgate was not merely a treasury of fact and wisdom, but a norm of speech. The Christian poetry antecedent to the Conquest exhibits a curious blending of ancient Germanic with Hebraic idiom, to which must be added a few Latin elements. The prose of Ælfred and Ælfric could not be otherwise than powerfully affected by the books which they were constantly obliged to quote or imitate. At intervals during the Old English period, translations were made from the Gospels, the Psalms, and other portions of the Scriptures. Bede was at work on a rendering of John's Gospel when he died, and more than two centuries later new versions, or recensions of older versions, were seeing the light. Theological activity, far from ceasing at the Conquest, was rather stimulated into new and more vigorous life. The era of cathedral building began, and much about the same time the first Miracle Plays must have been written. The tradition continues through such men as Orm, Richard of Hampole, and Langland, until we reach Wyclif — not even Chaucer lying outside its pale. From Wyclif to our own day the line is again unbroken. Who needs to be reminded of Tyndale, of Latimer, of Cromwell and his Puritans, of Bunyan, Addison, and Wesley? The Bible has been an active force in English literature for over twelve hundred years, and during that whole period it has been molding the diction of representative thinkers and literary artists. Forced into rivalry with other models, it has struggled against them, — now vanquished for the moment, now sharing with its competitors the trophies of conquest, and now sole master of the field, yet always most powerful when the national life was most intense, and scarcely ever so baffled but that some signs of its authority are manifest.

Before considering the nature of the *plastic* influence which the Bible has exercised upon English style, it may be well to remind ourselves of some of the more obvious ways in which Scriptural language has been appropriated by English writers. Of these the most important are direct quotation and allusion.

Under the head of direct quotation it will not be necessary to include the use made of Scripture in sermons and theological treatises; it will be sufficient to refer to its occasional employment by secular writers to produce the effect of impressiveness or pathos. This effect has been aptly characterized in the current number of an American periodical, by an author[1] whom I rejoice to call my friend. His words are, "A felicitous use of Scriptural quotations, with the solemn dignity of their style and feeling, brings us with our narrow cares into the presence of past ages,

---

[1] Rev. Frederic Palmer, in the *Andover Review* for April, 1892.

and raises the individual from his solitariness into union with man everywhere, with the infinite and the eternal."

This truth is akin to that recognized by Shakespeare and the great dramatists of antiquity, that tragedy requires the occasional introduction of the aphorism or gnomic sentence. The same principle holds in prose, though perhaps its application is here somewhat more limited. John Morley perceives its validity when he says of Burke: " Burke will always be read with delight and edification, because in the midst of discussions on the local and the accidental he scatters apothegms that take us into the regions of lasting wisdom. In the midst of the torrent of the most strenuous and passionate deliverances, he suddenly rises aloof from his immediate subject, and in all tranquillity reminds us of some permanent relation of things, some enduring truth of human life or society."[1] If a writer is sufficient for the coinage of his own maxims, it may in general be best that he should confine himself to these, especially where it is the pure intellect that is addressed; but if the sensibility is to be touched as well, a felicitous use of Scriptural phraseology will hardly fail to stir the deepest springs of emotion. Who has not been thrilled, even to tears, by the organ note struck at the euthanasia of Sydney Carton?

> She kisses his lips; he kisses hers; they solemnly bless each other. The spare hand does not tremble as he releases it; nothing worse than a sweet, bright constancy is in the patient face. She goes next before him — is gone; the knitting-women count Twenty-two.
>
> *I am the Resurrection and the Life, saith the Lord; he that believeth in me, though he were dead, yet shall he live; and whosoever liveth and believeth in me shall never die.*
>
> The murmuring of many voices, the upturning of many faces, the pressing on of many footsteps in the outskirts of the crowd, so that it swells forward in a mass, like one great heave of water, all flashes away. Twenty-three.
>
> They said of him, about the city that night, that it was the peacefulest man's face ever beheld there. Many added that he looked sublime and prophetic.

We might be tempted to believe that the emotion was created by the circumstances, or by Dickens' exquisite art in the shap-

---

[1] See also Aristotle's *Rhetoric*, Bk. 2, chap. 21.

ing of his own sentences; but read the final chapter without the Scripture words, and the difference will be readily appreciated.

Akin to direct quotation, but not identical with it, is the heightening of style through the employment of Biblical allusion. An instance of remote allusion is given by Payne, among the comments which follow.[1] A more palpable one is supplied by an apostrophe near the end of Shelley's *Defense of Poetry*.

> Their errors have been weighed and found to have been dust in the balance; if their sins were as scarlet, they are now white as snow; they have been washed in the blood of the mediator and redeemer, Time. Observe in what a ludicrous chaos the imputations of real or fictitious crime have been confused in the contemporary calumnies against poetry and poets; consider how little is as it appears — or appears as it is; look to your own motives, and judge not, lest ye be judged.

Here there are no fewer than seven Biblical sentences woven into a tissue all palpitating with generous sympathy and generous indignation.

Similar effects are often to be noted in poetry. Thus from the close of *Aurora Leigh:*

> He turned instinctively, — where, faint and far,
> Along the tingling desert of the sky,
> Beyond the circle of the conscious hills,
> Were laid in jasper-stone as clear as glass
> The first foundations of that new, near Day
> Which should be builded out of heaven to God.

Or from Longfellow's *Interlude* before the *Theologian's Tale:*

> Not to one church alone, but seven,
> The voice prophetic spake from heaven;
> And unto each the promise came,
> Diversified, but still the same;
> For him that overcometh are
> The new name written on the stone,
> The raiment white, the crown, the throne,
> And I will give him the Morning Star!

But our concern is with prose, not poetry, and in prose there are all grades and settings of allusion, down to the sheerest flip-

---

[1] See p. xxxvi.

pancy, even the latter testifying, through its very irreverence, to the arrowy momentum and tenacity of these winged words.

As instances of an average sort of allusion, remarkable neither for elevation nor smartness, I select two or three from a single volume of Matthew Arnold's essays (the italics are mine).

He [Wordsworth] is one of the very chief glories of English Poetry; and by nothing is England so glorious as by her poetry. *Let us lay aside every weight* which hinders our getting him recognized as this.

What we have of Shelley in poetry and prose suited with this charming picture of him; Mrs. Shelley's account suited with it; it was a possession which one would gladly have kept unimpaired. It still subsists, I must now add; it subsists even after one has read the present biography; it subsists, *but so as by fire.*

It [society] looked in Byron's glass as it looks in Lord Beaconsfield's, and sees, or fancies that it sees, *its own face there; and then it goes its way, and straightway forgets what manner of man it saw.*

When a writer, with a native vigor, lightness, and rapidity of his own, has become wholly permeated, as it were, with the thought and diction of the Bible, so that he has acquired its tone and manner, and yet kept himself above the condition of the mere servile and mechanical copyist, we have from him such a clear, simple, and picturesque *style as that of Bunyan.* Such writing has an archaic flavor, yet is intelligible to the meanest capacity; may be full of quotation, yet perfectly assimilates all that it quotes; abounds in allusion which it never degrades; but is best in that it seems to have drawn from the same perennial fountains as the Bible itself, instead of merely standing to it in a dependent and derivative relation. One or two familiar extracts from Bunyan will serve as illustrations.

As I walked through the wilderness of this world, I lighted on a certain place, where was a Den; and I laid me down in that place to sleep: and as I slept I dreamed a Dream. I dreamed, and behold I saw a man clothed with Rags, standing in a certain place, with his face from his own House, a Book in his hand, and a great burden upon his back. I looked, and saw him open the book, and read therein; and as he read, he wept and trembled; and not being able longer to contain, he brake out with a lamentable cry, saying, What shall I do?

Now I saw in my Dream that these two men went in at the Gate; and lo, as they entered, they were transfigured, and they had Raiment put on that shone like Gold. There were also that met them with Harps and Crowns, and gave them to them, the Harp to praise withal, and the Crowns in token of honor. Then I heard in my Dream that all the Bells in the City Rang again for joy, and that it was said unto them, Enter ye into the joy of your Lord. I also heard the men themselves, that they sang with a loud voice, saying, Blessing, Honor, Glory, and Power be to Him that sitteth upon the Throne, and to the Lamb for ever and ever.

In such examples as these we can study the Biblical style to better advantage, perhaps, than in the Bible itself. While preserving the essential qualities of Hebraic diction, Bunyan presents them at one remove from antiquity and its aloofness. Bunyan is a man of our own race, living but yesterday, as it were, in comparison with the centuries which separate us from the authors of the Bible. Moreover, in studying Bunyan we are not only studying Biblical style in English, but we are studying English itself at an epoch when, according to one of the most accomplished of foreign critics, it reached its best estate. Let us hear what Villemain has to say upon this topic. The time he is speaking of is the Restoration, and of it he affirms:[1] "English idiom then attained its happiest epoch; it was taking on refinement without becoming impoverished; it still, like the ancient Northern languages, had its whole rich supply of native, energetic, concise expressions. With these it had blended a strong tincture of Biblical imagination. Besides, though it appropriated in passing many French words, it only employed them, so to speak, as proper names and fashionable phrases, and in no respect changed the primitive originality of its exact and elliptical constructions, and the energy of its numberless metaphors. In this respect it did not model itself upon less regular and less poetic tongues; it remained in possession of its own physiognomy and of all its vigor."

We now approach our subject proper. What is the literary quality which the Bible possesses, and which it has therefore been communicating to English for nearly thirteen hundred years? In

---

[1] *Tableau de la littérature au XVIIIe Siècle*, I. 88.

asking this question, we refer to the Bible as if it were a single book, instead of being, as its very name signifies, a collection of books, each with its own peculiarities, and differing as widely as an impassioned lyric from a mere genealogy, as the detached aphorisms of the Book of Proverbs from the intricate arguments of the Epistles by Paul. But the term is convenient, and, after all, there is little danger of misunderstanding. Every one recognizes the main characteristics of Bible diction in general, though he may never have been at the pains to define to himself just what those characteristics are. To my mind they may be summed up in a very brief phrase. Whatever their number or variety, I think they may all be comprehended under a single term, noble naturalness.

But the phrase, noble naturalness, may be vague enough to stand in need of further definition. By 'natural' in its application to men and women, and the books which concern men and women, I mean 'conformable to human nature,' and by 'unnatural,' 'contrary to human nature, either in whole or in part.' Human nature may, for this purpose, be regarded as made up of sensibility, intellect, imagination, and will. A book whose arguments are an insult to intelligence is unnatural; but so is also, in some sense, a book which does not address the intellect at all. The latter sort of book may be called unnatural through defect. With this qualification, no book can be said to be thoroughly natural which does not address the whole man. The predominance of any one element of human nature to the virtual exclusion of the rest is sufficient, in a man or a book, to constitute a kind of unnaturalness. It is in this sense, therefore, that the Bible possesses eminent naturalness, as I shall attempt to show more at length in the sequel; and if to this naturalness be added an accent of dignity or elevation, the product will be what I have called noble naturalness.

Matthew Arnold has devoted a large part of his admirable essay *On Translating Homer* to the proof and elucidation of four statements concerning the style of Homer. In one place, by way of summary, he says: "Homer is rapid in his movement, Homer is plain in his words and style, Homer is simple in his ideas, Homer is noble in his manner." An expansion of his thought is found in another passage, as follows: "The translator of Homer should above all be penetrated by a sense of four qualities of his author; — that he is eminently rapid; that he is eminently plain and direct, both in the evolution of his thought and in the expression of it, that is, both in his syntax and in his words; that he is eminently plain and direct in the substance of his thought, that is, in his matter and ideas; and finally that he is eminently noble."

Let us assume that the fact is as Matthew Arnold alleges, and that, viewed in relation to most authors, Homer's narrative is uniformly rapid, plain, simple, and noble. How does the Homeric narrative compare in these respects with those of the Bible? Evidently it is with respect to narrative that Homer and the Bible should be compared, if they are compared at all, for it is this department of literature that Homer represents. For the answer to this question I may refer to Chateaubriand's parallel on p. lxiii. I do this with the more confidence, as I am assured by my colleague, Professor Seymour, whose authority on the subject of Homer is not likely to be impugned on this side of the Atlantic, that Chateaubriand has in no respect misrepresented the Homeric style, and that an objection on this score cannot be made to lie against his paraphrase of the verses from Ruth. But, leaving Chateaubriand's parallel out of consideration, and appealing to the consciousness of what the old Morality calls Everyman, did any one ever think a New Testament parable too long, too involved, or too mean? Did any one ever think so of any Gospel narrative whatever, of the Offering of Isaac by Abraham, or the Story of Joseph?

Here, then, we might rest the claim for the noble naturalness of the Biblical style. What can be more natural than that which, without demanding conscious effort, calls up a grateful echo in the heart of every man, and offends no one by the excess of any quality in itself good?

But to pursue the subject somewhat further into detail. I have referred above to a division of human nature into sensibility, intellect, imagination, and will. To each of these corresponds a species of writing which is addressed to it, and constitutes its aliment. Thus mathematics, and philosophy viewed in one aspect, appeal chiefly to the intellect; certain kinds of poetry affect almost exclusively the sensibilities, or the imagination, or both conjointly. Again, exhortations to resolve and action are primarily directed at the will, though they may call in the aid of the allied faculties. French critics, particularly those of the classical school, are wont to assert that in French literature the intellect, or reason, is supreme, other faculties being kept in strict subordination to this one. In Carlyle, on the other hand, we might say that the pure intellect is somewhat in abeyance; in much of Shelley's verse that both the intellect and the will are comparatively disregarded. With the Bible it is otherwise. Speaking broadly, it is pervaded at once by a rational element, a sensuous element, an imaginative element, and an animating or motive element. It is the union of these in due proportions which constitutes full and perfect naturalness, and such union we have in many parts of the Bible.

The Scriptures everywhere postulate intellect — or the absence of it; but only in a small minority of instances is it dealt with in what may be called the way of argument, or reasoning. There is no attempt to convert men from their errors by ratiocinative or philosophical processes. A right state of mind is denoted by such words as understanding, or wisdom. This is conceived as the direct gift of God, and connotes much besides clearness of intellectual vision. To the perfection of wisdom a right state of the will and affections is assumed as necessary, and thus we are led back to a consideration of human nature in its totality.

The presence of imagination in the Bible will need no proof. Who that has read the Psalms, or the Prophets, or the Apocalypse, can doubt it for a moment? And who will have any more hesitation in recognizing that the guidance of the will is perhaps the primary purpose which underlies history and precept, proverb, hymn, and vision of seer?

The sensuous element is perceptible in the metaphoric language and in the rhythm. However lofty or sublime be the sentiment, the diction is concrete, never abstract. Every chapter — with comparatively few exceptions — is a gallery of word-pictures; and it is this picturesqueness which makes the Bible always attractive and usually intelligible. To the great bulk of readers the abstract is identical with the dry, and but few persons could be won to a perusal, much less imitation, of the Bible, were it couched in the phraseology of an Aristotle. The picturesqueness of Scriptural language addresses the mind's eye; its simple, regular, natural harmony addresses the ear. Its harmony is simple, because it depends mainly on parallelism, or, as it has been called, antiphony; with this may be contrasted the intricate symphonic effects of a Pindaric ode, or of its most felicitous imitations in English, and, in prose, the now accelerated, now delayed and regressive footing of a prolonged Ciceronian period. It is regular, because the ear, when ever so little accustomed to it, knows just what to expect. The verses fall into a march-tune; their movement is disciplinary, first of the emotions, and through them of life and conduct. It is natural, because the emphatic syllable of the word — and this alike in Hebrew and English — coincides with the natural stress of the rhythm, and both with the pulse of the thought itself. In other words, that syllable which is fullest of meaning gets at the same time the rhythmical stroke within the word and within the verse. If this principle be compared with the quantitative laws of Latin and Greek — which apply to the harmonies of prose no less than to those of poetry — the difference will be apparent. Moreover, the balance of clauses is natural in another sense, in that their length coincides approximately with that of a single expiration of the breath. And this, as it is closely related with the pulse of the blood, with the beat of the heart, elucidates and justifies the remark of Dean Stanley, in his *History of the Jewish Church* (2. 165) : "'The rapid stroke as of alternate wings,' 'the heaving and sinking as of the troubled heart,' which have been beautifully described as the essence of the parallel structure of Hebrew verses, are exactly suited for the endless play of human feeling, and for the understanding of every age and nation."

The difference between the simplicity and directness of the Bible and the more complex and involved structure of Greek prose may be shown by comparing the close of a Thucydidean speech, being about one-sixth of Brasidas' harangue to his soldiers before their engagement with the Illyrians (Thuc. 4. 126), with the whole of Gideon's address to his men before their encounter with the Midianites (Judges 7. 17, 18).

If you repel their tumultuous onset, and, when opportunity offers, withdraw again in good order, keeping your ranks, you will sooner arrive at a place of safety, and will also learn the lesson that mobs like these, if an adversary withstand their first attack, do but threaten at a distance and make a flourish of valor, although if he yields to them they are quick enough to show their courage in following at his heels when there is no danger.

Look on me, and do likewise; and behold, when I come to the outside of the camp, it shall be that, as I do, so shall ye do.

When I blow with a trumpet, I and all that are with me, then blow ye the trumpets also on every side of all the camp, and say, The sword of the Lord, and of Gideon.

For purposes of comparison I add another speech, the prophecy of Jahaziel from 2 Chron. 20. 15-17, merely modernizing the punctuation in order that the resemblance of its sentence structure to that of a favorite species of nineteenth century English may be more apparent.

Hearken ye, all Judah, and ye inhabitants of Jerusalem, and thou king Jehoshaphat. Thus saith the LORD unto you: Be not afraid nor dismayed by reason of this great multitude, for the battle is not yours, but God's. To-morrow go ye down against them. Behold, they come up by the cliff of Ziz, and ye shall find them at the end of the brook, before the wilderness of Jeruel. Ye shall not need to fight in this battle. Set yourselves, stand ye still, and see the salvation of the LORD with you, O Judah and Jerusalem. Fear not, nor be dismayed. To-morrow go out against them, for the LORD will be with you.

Sensibility, we have seen, has a large place assigned it in the Bible. Every emotion is comprised in the mighty gamut. Is it friendship? Behold the love of David for Jonathan. Is it righteous anger? Consider the imprecations of the Psalmist. Is it exultation? Read over the Song of Deborah. Is it reverence, joy, hope, faith, grief, pity? Each one finds a tongue, and speaks the expressive language of the heart. How should the qualities of strength, vigor, simplicity, pathos, sublimity, be absent from compositions such as these? How should there be room for the intrusion of a frigid artificiality?

Artificiality is a sign that intellect has become a usurper on the domain of her rivals. It is a sign that, under pretence of issuing in a more presentable form the crude data furnished by nature and the human heart, the intellect has mangled, and mingled, and disguised them beyond recognition. It is not to the Bible, then, that we must look for artificiality, whether in the form of bombast, of empty declamation, or of supersubtle and wiredrawn conceits. Here is life; here is nature; nor is it matter for regret that, compared with the average endowment of the race, it is a higher life, a *melior natura*.

To turn now to the manifestation of some of these qualities in English style. Evidently there must be many cases in which it would be impossible to determine whether, when they appear in an English author, they have been immediately derived from converse with the Bible, or from familiarity with authors who directly, or through some intermediary, have drawn them from that source, or whether, in fine, they may have originated sporadically, as it were, and have accidentally, or rather most naturally, coincided and blended with the same qualities already in process of dissemination from this one grand reservoir.

In the following passage from Macaulay's *Essay on Milton*, it will perhaps be conceded that he is Hebraizing, at least in part.

> He prostrated himself in the dust before his Maker; but he set his foot on the neck of his king. In his devotional retirement he prayed with convulsions, and groans, and tears. He was half maddened by glorious or terrible illusions. He heard the lyres of angels or the tempting whispers of fiends. He caught a gleam of the Beatific Vision, or woke screaming from dreams of everlasting fire. Like Vane, he thought himself intrusted with the sceptre of the millennial year. Like Fleetwood, he cried in the bitterness of his soul that God had hid his face from him. . . . The intensity of their feelings on one subject made them tranquil on every other. One overpowering sentiment had subjected to itself pity and hatred, ambition and fear. Death had lost its terrors, and pleasure its charms.

The kind of sentence-structure illustrated by this extract has been called constructive or artificial, in contradistinction to another known as the cumulative. Much of Milton's prose is in the latter style. Of the former Payne says (Introduction to Burke's *Select Works*, Vol. I.) : "The modern or French method is to unite the members of the passage by a connexion of ideas; as Dr. Whately expresses it, 'to interweave or rather *felt* them together,' by making the thought pass over from one member to the other; by concealing the sutures, and making the parts fit into and complement each other. This method leaves better opportunities for marking boldly the transitions in the argument, and, if appropriate, making corresponding changes in the style."

Now this 'modern or French method' probably owes something to the epistolary style of Cicero, something to the Latinity of the silver age, something to Biblical models, and something to an artistic striving after inartificiality, a pursuit of the analytic and simple, in avoidance of the synthetic and complex. The severance in the literary product between what is due to one and what to another of these causes will often be extremely difficult, if not impossible. In the subjoined extract from Addison's *Vision of Mirzah*, however, the nature of the subject and the general mode of treatment make the task easier, and lead to the conclusion that it certainly owes much to Scriptural suggestion.

He then led me to the highest pinnacle of the rock, and placed me on the top of it. Cast thy eyes eastward, said he, and tell me what thou seest. I see, said I, a huge valley and a prodigious tide of water rolling through it. The valley that thou seest, said he, is the vale of misery, and the tide of water that thou seest is part of the great tide of eternity. What is the reason, said I, that the tide I see rises out of a thick mist at one end, and again loses itself in a thick mist at the other? What thou seest, said he, is that portion of eternity which is called time, measured out by the sun, and reaching from the beginning of the world to its consummation. Examine now, said he, this sea that is thus bounded with darkness at both ends, and tell me what thou discoverest in it. I see a bridge, said I, standing in the midst of the tide. The bridge thou seest, said he, is human life; consider it attentively. Upon a more leisurely survey of it, I found that it consisted of threescore and ten entire arches, with several broken arches, which, added to those that were entire, made up the number about an hundred.

The archaic style of parts of the *Urn Burial* suggests a similar pattern, as a glance at this passage will show.

> The dead seem all alive in the human Hades of Homer, yet cannot well speak, prophesy, or know the living, except they drink blood, wherein is the life of man. And therefore the souls of Penelope's paramours, conducted by Mercury, chirped like bats, and those which followed Hercules made a noise but like a flock of birds. The departed spirits know things past and to come, yet are ignorant of things present. Agamemnon foretells what should happen unto Ulysses, yet ignorantly inquires what is become of his own son. The ghosts are afraid of swords in Homer; yet Sibylla tells Æneas in Virgil, the thin habit of spirits was beyond the force of weapons.

But it is when we come to authors like Hume, Hazlitt, or Lamb, that we are more in doubt. What shall we say in this respect of paragraphs like the following?

> The Grecian addressed himself to an audience much less refined than the Roman senate or judges. The lowest vulgar of Athens were his sovereigns and the arbiters of his eloquence. Yet is his manner more chaste and austere than that of the other. Could it be copied, its success would be infallible over a modern assembly. It is rapid harmony, exactly adjusted to the sense. It is vehement reasoning, without any appearance of art. It is disdain, anger, boldness, freedom, involved in a continual stream of argument. And of all human productions, the orations of Demosthenes present to us the models which approach the nearest to perfection.

> But I may say of him here, that he is the only person I ever knew who answered to the idea of a man of genius. He is the only person from whom I ever learnt anything. There is only one thing he could learn from me in return, but *that* he has not. He was the first poet I ever knew. His genius at that time had angelic wings, and fed on manna. He talked on for ever; and you wished him to talk on for ever. His thoughts did not seem to come with labor and effort, but as if borne on the gusts of genius, and as if the wings of his imagination lifted him from off his feet. His voice rolled on the ear like the pealing organ, and its sound alone was the music of thought. His mind was clothed with wings; and raised on them, he lifted philosophy to heaven.

> My reading has been lamentably desultory and immethodical. Odd, out of the way, old English plays and treatises, have supplied me with most of my notions and ways of feeling. In everything that relates to *science*, I am a whole Encyclopædia behind the rest of the world. I should have scarcely

cut a figure among the franklins, or country gentlemen, in King John's days. I know less geography than a schoolboy of six weeks' standing. To me a map of old Ortelius is as authentic as Arrowsmith.

The first of these is from a discourse on Eloquence, by Hume, the second, Hazlitt's opinion on Coleridge, from his *English Poets*, and the third from *Elia* (*The Old and the New Schoolmaster*). They are all in the constructive or artificial style, and, so far as syntax goes, have much in common with the Bible. It may be urged that their authors are quite as likely to be imitators of Seneca, or of his imitators. But, apart from the question whether Seneca himself may not have come under Hebraic influence, it must still be said that the ear of the English reader (and it is for the reader that, after all has been said, style is elaborated) had been attuned, not by the treatises On Anger and On Benefits, but by the cadences of Scripture. If now we compare these citations with examples of the cumulative style, the difference will be most conspicuous. The first extract which follows is from Hooker's *Ecclesiastical Polity* (Bk. I. Chap. 3), the second from Milton's *Of Reformation in England*, near its close.

But we must further remember also (which thing to touch in a word shall suffice) that as in this respect they have their law, which law directeth them in the means whereby they tend to their own perfection, so likewise another law there is, which toucheth them as they are sociable parts united into one body, a law which bindeth them each to serve unto other's good, and all to prefer the good of the whole before whatsoever their own particular, as we plainly see they do when things natural in that regard forget their ordinary natural wont, that which is heavy mounting sometime upwards of its own accord, and forsaking the centre of the earth, which to itself is most natural, even as if it did hear itself commanded to let go the good it privately wisheth, and to relieve the present distress of nature in common.

Then, amidst the hymns and hallelujahs of saints, some one may perhaps be heard offering at high strains in new and lofty measure to sing and celebrate thy divine mercies and marvelous judgments in this land throughout all ages; whereby this great and warlike nation, instructed and inured to the fervent and continual practice of truth and righteousness, and casting far from her the rags of her whole vices, may press on hard to that high and happy emulation to be found the soberest, wisest, and most Christian people at that day when thou, the eternal and shortly expected King, shalt open the clouds to judge the several kingdoms of the world, and, distributing national honors and rewards to religious and just commonwealths, shalt put an end to all earthly tyrannies, proclaiming thy universal and mild monarchy through heaven and earth, where they undoubtedly that by their labors, counsels, and prayers have been earnest for the common good of religion and their country, shall receive, above the inferior orders of the blessed, the regal addition of principalities, legions, and thrones into their glorious titles, and in supereminence of beatific vision progressing the dateless and irrevoluble circle of eternity, shall clasp inseparable hands with joy and bliss, in overmeasure for ever.

Who could mistake these, though the latter is colored by Scriptural phrases, for imitations of Scriptural style, or regard them as conformable to it?[1] In its simplicity and concreteness *Robinson Crusoe* has much more in common with the Bible, and it is from this source that those qualities were no doubt in large measure derived. Let us see.

I found also that the island I was in was barren, and, as I saw good reason to believe, uninhabited, except by wild beasts, of whom however I saw none. Yet I saw abundance of fowls, but knew not their kinds; neither when I killed them could I tell what was fit for food, and what not. At my coming back I shot at a great bird which I saw sitting upon a tree on the side of a great wood. I believe it was the first gun that had been fired there since the creation of the world. I had no sooner fired but from all the parts of the wood there arose an innumerable number of fowls of many sorts, making a confused screaming, and crying every one according to his usual note, but not one of them of any kind that I knew. As for the creature I killed, I took it to be a kind of a hawk, its color and beak resembling it, but had no talons or claws more than common. Its flesh was carrion, and fit for nothing.

But the matter is beyond dispute when we come to a piece of classic prose like Lincoln's Second Inaugural, which certainly owes nothing to the Romans (oftener Spaniards) of the Decadence.

Neither party expected for the war the magnitude or the duration which it has already attained. Neither anticipated that the cause of the conflict might cease with, or even before, the conflict itself should cease. Each looked for an easier triumph, and a result less fundamental and astounding. Both read the same Bible, and pray to the same God; and each invokes his aid against

---

[1] They rather suggest Cicero as an ultimate model.

the other. It may seem strange that any men should dare to ask a just God's assistance in wringing their bread from the sweat of other men's faces; but let us judge not, that we be not judged. The prayers of both could not be answered. That of neither has been answered fully. The Almighty has his own purposes.

At this point we may pause, for we need no further demonstration of the indebtedness of English prose style to the Bible, nor would it be easy to discover a better illustration of Biblical qualities in modern guise, exemplified in a passage of more interest to all the world. South reckoned it a mark of illiteracy to be fond of 'high-flown metaphors and allegories, attended and set off with scraps of Greek and Latin.' If this be true, the American people in so far escape the imputation as they have set the seal of their approval on such writing as Lincoln's; and that they have had the judgment and taste to do so is due, more than to any other cause, to their familiarity with the Bible.[1]

---

[1] For a parallel influence of the Bible on German cf. Nägelsbach's remarks in his *Lateinische Stilistik*, p. 7: " Während nun in den Schulen diese grösstentheils brotlosen Künste getrieben wurden und das Latein so sehr seine Würde verlor, dass es vor hundert Jahren in Deutschland wohl schwerlich mehr als drei geschmackvolle Stilisten gab, Mosheim, Gesner und Ernesti, *hob sich auf der andern Seite die Muttersprache, an die rein gebliebene Kirchen- und Bibelsprache anknüpfend, zu einer nie geahnten Darstellungsfähigkeit.*"

ILLUSTRATIVE COMMENTS.

1. Importance of the Bible to the Student of English.

[RUSKIN, *Præterita*, Chap. 1.]

WALTER SCOTT and Pope's Homer were reading of my own selection, but my mother forced me, by steady daily toil, to learn long chapters of the Bible by heart; as well as to read it every syllable through, aloud, hard names and all, from Genesis to the Apocalypse, about once a year; and to that discipline — patient, accurate, and resolute — I owe, not only a knowledge of the book, which I find occasionally serviceable, but much of my general power of taking pains, and the best part of my taste in literature. From Walter Scott's novels I might easily, as I grew older, have fallen to other people's novels; and Pope might, perhaps, have led me to take Johnson's English, or Gibbon's, as types of language; but, once knowing the 32nd of Deuteronomy, the 119th Psalm, the 15th of 1st Corinthians, the Sermon on the Mount, and most of the Apocalypse, every syllable by heart, and having always a way of thinking with myself what words meant, it was not possible for me, even in the foolishest times of youth, to write entirely superficial or formal English.

[RUSKIN, *Præterita*, Chap. 2.]

I have next with deeper gratitude to chronicle what I owed to my mother for the resolutely consistent lessons which so exercised me in the Scriptures as to make every word of them familiar to my ear in habitual music, — yet in that familiarity reverenced, as transcending all thought, and ordaining all conduct.

This she effected, not by her own sayings or personal authority; but simply by compelling me to read the book thoroughly, for myself. As soon as I was able to read with fluency, she began a course of Bible work with me, which never ceased till I went to Oxford. She read alternate verses with me, watching, at first, every intonation of my voice, and correcting the false ones, till she made me understand the verse, if within my reach, rightly, and energetically. It might be beyond me altogether; that she did not care about; but she made sure that as soon as I got hold of it at all, I should get hold of it by the right end.

In this way she began with the first verse of Genesis, and went straight through, to the last verse of the Apocalypse; hard names, numbers, Levitical law, and all; and began again at Genesis the next day. If a name was hard, the better the exercise in pronunciation,— if a chapter was tiresome, the better lesson in patience, — if loathsome, the better lesson in faith that there was some use in its being so outspoken. After our chapters, (from two to three a day, according to their length, the first thing after breakfast, and no interruption from servants allowed, — none from visitors, who either joined in the reading or had to stay upstairs, — and none from any visitings or excursions, except real traveling,) I had to learn a few verses by heart, or repeat, to make sure I had not lost, something of what was already known; and, with the chapters thus gradually possessed from the first word to the last, I had to learn the whole body of the fine old Scottish paraphrases, which are good, melodious, and forceful verse; and to which, together with the Bible itself, I owe the first cultivation of my ear in sound.

It is strange that of all the pieces of the Bible which my mother thus taught me, that which cost me most to learn, and which was, to my child's mind, chiefly repulsive — the 119th Psalm — has now become of all the most precious to me. . . .

But it is only by deliberate effort that I recall the long morning hours of toil, as regular as sunrise, — toil on both sides equal — by which, year after year, my mother forced me to learn these paraphrases, and chapters, (the eighth of 1st Kings being one —

try it, good reader, in a leisure hour!) allowing not so much as a syllable to be missed or misplaced; while every sentence was required to be said over and over again till she was satisfied with the accent of it. I recollect a struggle between us of about three weeks, concerning the accent of the 'of' in the lines

> Shall any following spring revive
> The ashes of the urn? —

I insisting, partly in childish obstinacy, and partly in true instinct for rhythm, (being wholly careless on the subject both of urns and their contents,) on reciting it with an accented *of*. It was not, I say, till after three weeks' labor, that my mother got the accent lightened on the 'of' and laid on the ashes, to her mind. But had it taken three years, she would have done it, having once undertaken to do it. And, assuredly, had she not done it, — well, there's no knowing what would have happened; but I'm very thankful she *did*.

I have just opened my oldest (in use) Bible, — a small, closely, and very neatly printed volume it is, printed in Edinburgh by Sir D. Hunter Blair and J. Bruce, Printers to the King's Most Excellent Majesty, in 1816. Yellow, now, with age, and flexible, but not unclean, with much use, except that the lower corners of the pages at 8th of 1st Kings, and 32d Deuteronomy, are worn somewhat thin and dark, the learning of these two chapters having cost me much pains. My mother's list of the chapters with which, thus learned, she established my soul in life, has just fallen out of it.

I will take what indulgence the incurious reader can give me, for printing the list thus accidentally occurrent: —

Exodus	chapters	15th and 20th.
2 Samuel	"	1st, from 17th verse to the end.
1 Kings	"	8th.
Psalms	"	{ 23d, 32d, 90th, 91st, 103d, 112th, 119th, 139th.
Proverbs	"	2d, 3d, 8th, 12th.
Isaiah	"	58th.

Matthew	chapters	5th, 6th, 7th.
Acts	"	26th.
1 Corinthians	"	13th, 15th.
James	"	4th.
Revelation	"	5th, 6th.

And truly, though I have picked up the elements of a little further knowledge — in mathematics, meteorology, and the like, in after life, — and owe not a little to the teaching of many people, this maternal installation of my mind in that property of chapters, I count very confidently the most precious, and, on the whole, the one *essential* part of all my education.

[MATTHEW ARNOLD, *Isaiah of Jerusalem*, pp. 4-5.]

I rate the value of the operation of poetry and literature upon men's minds extremely high; and from no poetry and literature, not even from our own Shakespeare and Milton, great as they are and our own as they are, have I, for my own part, received so much delight and stimulus as from Homer and Isaiah. To know, in addition to one's native literature, a great poetry and literature not of home growth, is an influence of the highest value; it very greatly widens one's range. The Bible has thus been an influence of the highest value for the nations of Christendom. And the effect of Hebrew poetry can be preserved and transferred in a foreign language, as the effect of other great poetry cannot. The effect of Homer, the effect of Dante, is and must be in great measure lost in a translation, because their poetry is a poetry of metre, or of rime, or both; and the effect of these is not really transferable. A man may make a good English poem with the matter and thoughts of Homer or Dante, may even try to reproduce their metre, or to reproduce their rime; but the metre and rime will be in truth his own, and the effect will be his, not the effect of Homer or Dante. Isaiah's, on the other hand, is a poetry, as is well known, of parallelism; it depends not on metre and rime, but on a balance of thought, conveyed by a corresponding balance of sentence; and the effect of this can be transferred to another language. Hebrew poetry has in addition the effect of assonance and other effects which cannot perhaps be transferred; but its main effect, its effect of parallelism of thought and sentence, can.

[BOWEN, *A Layman's Study of the English Bible*, Chap. I.]

Leaving these general considerations, let us now come to particulars, and consider that aspect of the study of the *English* Bible which makes it interesting to the mere lover of literature. Look first at the diction, and weigh its merits regarded simply as a specimen of English prose. The opinion of scholars is unanimous that its excellence in this respect is unmatched; English literature has nothing equal to it, and is indeed largely indebted to conscious or unconscious imitation of it for many of its best and most characteristic qualities. The diction is remarkable for clearness, simplicity, and strength. It is as simple and natural as the prattle of children at play, yet never lacking in grace or dignity, or in variety and expressive force. Till our attention is called to it, we seldom notice what I may call the homeliness of the style, the selection of short and pithy Saxon turns of expression, and the wealth and strength of idiomatic phrase. One who should attempt to imitate it would easily lapse into vulgar and colloquial language, or, in striving to avoid this fault, into a certain primness and stiffness of speech, which is even worse. In truth, it cannot be imitated; to write such prose as that of our Common Version is now one of the lost arts. And I have not yet mentioned what is to many persons the peculiar and most striking charm of the style; that is, its musical quality, the silvery ring of the sentences, and the rich and varied melody of its cadences whenever the sense comes to a close....

Now the century beginning about 1520, during which our English Bible thus gradually obtained its present beauty and finish, was precisely that in which our noble mother tongue completed its process of development and attained its highest stage of perfection. Since this period, there has been indeed an enlargement of its stores, in order to keep pace with the progress of science, invention, and art; but we witness no further process of organic growth. We see change, but no further amendment; rather a deterioration. This was the age of Hooker, Shakespeare, and Bacon; of Spenser, Latimer, and Raleigh; and it prepared the way for Hobbes and Dryden. It was the golden age of the English drama. These are great names, and many passages in their writings show a complete mastery of the English language, and form a grand display of its versatility, its sweetness, and its strength. But beside them all, and above them all, is the prose of our Common Version. It is more sustained than any of them, more uniformly strong and melodious in its flow, reminding one of the famous couplet of Denham on the Thames:—

> Though deep yet clear, though gentle yet not dull,
> Strong without rage, without o'erflowing full.

And it has largely contributed to the fixation of the language at this its best estate, since the number of words in it the meaning of which has become obsolete in the course of nearly three subsequent centuries is so small that they may almost be counted on the fingers. True, the diction seems often to have a slightly archaic tinge; but this is an advantage rather than a fault, as it tends to preserve the dignity and impressiveness of the style. . . .

I ought to cite specimens in justification of the high praise here awarded to the English style of the Bible. But one is at a loss what to choose out of the wealth of material at hand; and then, so much of the charm of passages from the Scriptures is due to associations going back to one's childhood, and to the intrinsic power and sweetness of the thought, the precept, or the sentiment, that it is hard to fasten our attention on the mere diction. But in what follows, let me ask the reader to divest his mind, if he can, from all thought of the doctrine conveyed, or of the tenderness and pathos of the sentiment, and to consider the felicity and the music of the words alone.

Come unto me, all ye that labor and are heavy laden, and I will give you rest. Take my yoke upon you, and learn of me; for I am meek and lowly in heart; and ye shall find rest unto your souls. For my yoke is easy, and my burden is light. — Matthew 11. 28-30.

Again : —

O Jerusalem, Jerusalem, thou that killest the prophets, and stonest them which are sent unto thee, how often would I have gathered thy children together, even as a hen gathereth her chickens under her wings, and ye would not! Behold, your house is left unto you desolate. For I say unto you, Ye shall not see me henceforth, till ye shall say, Blessed is he that cometh in the name of the Lord. — Matthew 23. 37-39.

Once more : —

For there is hope of a tree, if it be cut down, that it will sprout again, and that the tender branch thereof will not cease. Though the root thereof wax old in the earth, and the stock thereof die in the ground; yet through the scent of water it will bud, and bring forth boughs like a plant. But man dieth, and wasteth away; yea, man giveth up the ghost, and where is he? As the waters fail from the sea, and the flood decayeth and drieth up; so man lieth down and riseth not; till the heavens be no more, they shall not awake, nor be raised out of their sleep. — Job 14. 7-12.

Lastly : —

> I will take no bullock out of thy house,
> Nor he goats out of thy folds.
> For every beast of the forest is mine,
> And the cattle upon a thousand hills.
> Will I eat the flesh of bulls,
> Or drink the blood of goats?
> Offer unto God thanksgiving;
> And pay thy vows unto the Most High:
> And call upon me in the day of trouble :
> I will deliver thee, and thou shalt glorify me.
>
> Psalm 50. 9-15.

I may seem to have labored this point too much. But what is here said is particularly addressed to young students, since it may be supposed that one leading purpose of their education is the formation of a good prose style, at once clear and flowing, strong and pure. I hope to show that the proper study of the Bible may be, and ought to be, a means of comprehensive and thorough training, not only in theology, to which it is but too often exclusively devoted, and in philosophy, poetry, and history, but also in literature and English style. In any scheme of University studies, it is a great mistake to make over any one department altogether to mere specialists, and thereby to lead the mind of the student along one narrow track, strictly fenced in against any excursion over the other broad fields of human culture which lie around it on every side. Now this end, the formation of a good prose style, cannot be attained by precept and system, by conscious effort or the observance of fixed rules. But just as a man's character and conduct are mainly determined by the company that he keeps, so his modes of utterance are silently fashioned by unconscious imitation of the models which he has often before him, that is, by the books which he most familiarly reads. It is said of Voltaire, that he always had a copy of the 'Petit Carême' of Massillon lying on his writing-table, to be taken up during any odd quarter of an hour, for the sake of its influence on his style. The method was good, though perhaps the choice was not happy. I think Pascal, Rochefoucauld, or La Bruyère would have served his purpose better. But there can be no doubt what English models we ought to select. Keep the Bible, a volume of Shakespeare, and Lord Bacon's Essays always within arm's-reach; half an hour devoted to either of them will be mere recreation, and will never be unprofitably spent. Only when your minds and memories have become saturated with the prose of our Common Version, with the phraseology of Shakespeare, and even, if one has command of French, with the neat succinctness, precision, and point of Pascal, will you have mastered the elements of a good English style. Then only will you have a copious vocabulary to draw from, a rich store of words and phrases and a variety of allusions always at hand, and not be obliged painfully to ransack a meagre and hidebound diction in order to set forth your meaning. But as most people nowadays read little except the newspapers and ten-cent novels, one need not wonder that they talk and write slang, or adopt only a slipshod, stilted, or uncouth phraseology. Coleridge rightly says, in his Table-Talk, 'Intense study of the Bible will keep any writer from being *vulgar* in point of style.'

John Ruskin is certainly the greatest master that the present century has produced of pure, idiomatic, vigorous, and eloquent English prose; and as the first volume of his 'Modern Painters,' perhaps his best work, appeared over forty years ago, when he was a recent 'Graduate of Oxford,' his style was perfectly formed while he was yet a young man. How was it formed? In one of his latest writings he has told us that in his childhood, as a part of his home education, his mother required him to commit to memory, and repeat to her, passages from the Bible. A similar custom, as some of us old men know, prevailed here in New England over half a century ago, and I hope that in some families it lingers still. Ruskin gives us the exact list, twenty-six in number, of the Psalms and chapters which he thus learned by heart; and as the selection was in the main an excellent one, we need not seek further for the secret of his admirable diction and perfect command of English phraseology.

2. English Imitators of Biblical Language.

[VENABLES, *Biographical Introduction to Bunyan*, Clarendon Press Series, pp. xl–xli.]

The great charm of the *Pilgrim's Progress* is the purity, the homeliness, of its vernacular. Few were ever such complete masters of their 'sweet mother tongue' in its native vigor as Bunyan. The book stands unrivaled as a model of our English speech, plain but never vulgar, full of metaphor but never obscure, always intelligible, always forcible, going straight to the point in the fewest and simplest words. He is 'powerful and picturesque,' writes Mr. Hallam, 'from his concise simplicity.' Bunyan's style is recommended by Lord Macaulay as 'an invaluable study to every person who wishes to gain a wide command over the English language. Its vocabulary is the vocabulary of the common people. There is not an expression, if we except a few technical terms of theology, that would puzzle the rudest peasant.' He remarks that there are whole pages which do not contain a single word of more than two syllables, and that thus there is no book which shows so well 'how rich the old unpolluted English is in its proper wealth, and how little it has been improved by all that it has borrowed.' And the reason of this excellence is evident. Bunyan's English was the English of the Bible. By constant perusal his mind was thoroughly steeped in Holy Scripture; he thought its thoughts, spoke its words, adopted its images. 'In no book,' writes Mr. Green, 'do we see more clearly the new imaginative force which had been given to the common life of Englishmen by their study of the Bible. Its English is the simplest and homeliest English that has ever been used by any great English writer, but it is the English of the Bible.' Those who desire to become, like him, masters of our own grand mother tongue, and use it as an instrument for swaying the hearts, and elevating the souls, and instructing the minds of others, can take no better way to this end — to say nothing of its higher purposes — than to familiarize themselves, as he did, by constant perusal, with our English Bible.

[PAYNE, *Introduction to Burke, Select Works*, I. xxxv–xxxvi.]

There is a passage in the former [Burke's Address to the King] which Lord Grenville thought the finest that Burke ever wrote — perhaps the finest in the English language, — beginning, 'What, gracious Sovereign, is the empire of America to us, or the empire of the world, if we lose our own liberties?' which was evidently suggested by the passage in St. Matthew, 'What shall a man give in exchange for his soul?' In the sections of his works in which this grave simplicity is most prominent, Burke frequently employed the impressive phrases of the Holy Scriptures, affording a signal illustration of the truth that he neglects the most valuable repository of rhetoric in the English language who has not well studied the English Bible.

3. The King James Version.

[SAINTSBURY, *History of Elizabethan Literature*, Chap. 6.]

But great as are Bacon and Raleigh, they cannot approach, as writers of prose, the company of scholarly divines who produced — what is probably the greatest prose work in any language — the Authorized Version of the Bible in English. Now that there is at any rate some fear of this masterpiece ceasing to be what it has been for three centuries — the school and training ground of every man and woman of English speech in the noblest uses of English tongue — every one who values his mother tongue is more especially bound to put on record his own allegiance to it. . . .

The advantages which, in a manner at least, were peculiar to themselves, may be divided into two classes. They were in the very centre of the great literary ferment of which in this volume I am striving to give a history as little inadequate as possible. They had in the air around them an English purged of archaisms and uncouthnesses, fully adapted to every literary purpose, and yet still racy of the soil, and free from that burden of hackneyed and outworn literary platitudes and commonplaces with which centuries of voluminous literary production have vitiated and loaded the English of our own day. They were not afraid of Latinizing, but they had an ample stock of the pure vernacular to draw on. These things may be classed together. On the other side, but equally healthful, may be put the fact that the style and structure of the originals and earlier versions, and especially that verse division which has been now so unwisely abandoned, served as safeguards against the besetting sin of all prose writers of their time, the habit of indulging in long wandering sentences, in paragraphs destitute of proportion and of grace, destitute even of ordinary manageableness and shape. The verses saved them from that once for all; while on the other hand their own taste, and the help given by the structure of the original in some cases, prevented them from losing sight of the wood for the trees, and omitting to consider the relation of verse to verse, as well as the antiphony of the clauses within the verse. Men without literary faculty might no doubt have gone wrong; but these were men of great literary faculty, whose chief liabilities to error were guarded against precisely by the very conditions in which they found their work. The hour had come exactly, and so for once had the men.

The result of their labors is so universally known that it is not necessary to say very much about it; but the mere fact of the universal knowledge carries with it a possibility of under-valuation. In another place, dealing with the general subject of English prose style, I have selected the sixth and seventh verses of the eighth chapter of Solomon's Song as the best example known to me of absolutely perfect English prose — harmonious, modulated, yet in no sense trespassing the limits of prose and becoming poetry. I have in the same place selected, as a companion passage from a very different original, the Charity passage of the First Epistle to the Corinthians. . . .

The days of creation; the narratives of Joseph and his brethren, of Ruth, of the final defeat of Ahab, of the discomfiture of the Assyrian host of Sennacherib; the moral discourses of Ecclesiastes and Ecclesiasticus and the Book of Wisdom; the poems of the Psalms and the Prophets; the visions of the Revelation, — a hundred other passages which it is unnecessary to catalogue, — will always be the *ne plus ultra* of English composition in their several kinds, and the storehouse from which generation after generation of writers, sometimes actually hostile to religion and often indifferent to it, will draw the materials, and not unfrequently the actual form, of their most impassioned and elaborate passages. . . . The plays of Shakespeare and the English Bible are, and will ever be, the twin monuments not merely of their own period, but of the perfection of English, the complete expressions of the literary capacities of the language, at the time when it had lost none of its pristine vigor, and had put on enough but not too much of the adornments and the limitations of what may be called literary civilization.

[GREEN, *History of the English People,* Bk. 7, Chap. 1.]

Religion indeed was only one of the causes for this sudden popularity of the Bible. The book was equally important in its bearing on the intellectual development of the people. All the prose literature of England, save the forgotten tracts of Wyclif, has grown up since the translation of the Scriptures by Tyndale and Coverdale. So far as the nation at large was concerned, no history, no romance, hardly any poetry save the little-known verse of Chaucer, existed in the English tongue when the Bible was ordered to be set up in churches. Sunday after Sunday, day after day, the crowds that gathered round the Bible in the nave of St. Paul's, or the family group that hung on its words in the devotional exercises at home, were leavened with a new literature. Legend and annal, war song and psalm, State-roll and biography, the mighty voices of prophets, the parables of Evangelists, stories of mission journeys, of perils by the sea and among the heathen, philosophic arguments, apocalyptic visions, all were flung broadcast over minds unoccupied for the most part by any rival learning. The disclosure of the stores of Greek literature had wrought the revolution of the Renascence. The disclosure of the older mass of Hebrew literature wrought the revolution of the Reformation. But the one revolution was far deeper and wider in its effects than the other. No version could transfer to another tongue the peculiar charm of language which gave their value to the authors of Greece and Rome. Classical letters therefore remained in the possession of the learned, that is, of the few; and among these, with the exception of Colet and More, or of the pedants who revived a Pagan worship in the gardens of the Florentine Academy, their direct influence was purely intellectual. But the language of the Hebrew, the idiom of the Hellenistic Greek, lent themselves with a curious felicity to the purposes of translation. As a mere literary monument, the English version of the Bible remains the noblest example of the English tongue, while its perpetual use made it, from the instant of its appearance, the standard of our language.

For the moment, however, its literary effect was less than its social. The power of the book over the mass of Englishmen showed itself in a thousand superficial ways, and in none more conspicuously than in the influence it exerted on ordinary speech. It formed, we must repeat, the whole literature which was practically accessible to ordinary Englishmen; and when we recall the number of common phrases which we owe to great authors, the bits of Shakespeare, or Milton, or Dickens, or Thackeray, which unconsciously interweave themselves in our ordinary talk, we shall better understand the strange mosaic of Biblical words and phrases which colored English talk two hundred years ago. The mass of picturesque allusion and illustration which we borrow from a thousand books, our fathers were forced to borrow from one; and the borrowing was the easier and the more natural that the range of the Hebrew literature fitted it for the expression of every phase of feeling. When Spenser poured forth his warmest love-notes in the 'Epithalamion,' he adopted the very words of the Psalmist, as he bade the gates open for the entrance of his bride. When Cromwell saw the mists break over the hills of Dunbar, he hailed the sunburst with the cry of David: 'Let God arise, and let his enemies be scattered. Like as the smoke vanisheth, so shalt thou drive them away!' Even to common minds this familiarity with grand poetic imagery in prophet and apocalypse gave a loftiness and ardor of expression that, with all its tendency to exaggeration and bombast, we may prefer to the slipshod vulgarisms of to-day.

[WILLIAM TYNDALE, *The Obedience of a Christian Man* (1528), Preface.]

The Greek tongue agreeth more with the English than with the Latin. And the properties of the Hebrew tongue agreeth a thousand times more with the English than with the Latin. The manner of speaking is both one, so that in a thousand places thou needest not but to translate it into the English word for word, when thou must seek a compass in the Latin, and yet shalt have much work to translate it well-favoredly, so that it have the same grace and sweetness, sense and pure understanding with it in the Latin and as it hath in the Hebrew. A thousand parts better may it be translated into the English than into the Latin.

[MARSH, *Lectures on the English Language*, Lectures 4 and 28.]

When an intelligent foreigner commences the study of English, he finds every page sprinkled with words whose form unequivocally betrays a Greek or Latin origin. . . . Further study would teach him that he had overrated the importance and relative amount of the foreign ingredients; that many of our seemingly insignificant and barbarous consonantal monosyllables are pregnant with the mightiest thoughts, and alive with the deepest feeling; that the language of the purposes and the affections, of the will and of the heart, is genuine English-born; that the dialect of the market and the fireside is Anglo-Saxon; that the vocabulary of the most impressive and effective pulpit orators has been almost wholly drawn from the same pure source; that the advocate who would convince the technical judge, or dazzle and confuse the jury, speaks Latin; while he who would touch the better sensibilities of his audience, or rouse the multitude to vigorous action, chooses his words from the native speech of our ancient fatherland; that the domestic tongue is a language of passion and persuasion, the foreign, of authority, or of rhetoric and debate; that we may not only frame single sentences, but speak for hours, without employing a single imported word; and finally that we possess the entire volume of divine revelation in the truest, clearest, aptest form in which human ingenuity has made it accessible to modern man, and yet with a vocabulary wherein, saving proper names and terms not in their nature translatable, scarce seven words in the hundred are derived from any foreign source. . . .

The general result of a comparison between the diction of the English Bible and that of the secular literature of England is that we have had, from the very dawn of our literature, a sacred and a profane dialect, the former eminently native, idiomatic, vernacular, and permanent, the latter composite, heterogeneous, irregular, and fluctuating; the one pure, natural, and expressive, the other mixed, and comparatively distorted and conventional. . . .

It will generally be found that the passages of the Received Version whose diction is most purely Saxon are not only most forcible in expression, but also the most faithful transcripts of the text, and that a Latinized style is seldom employed without loss of beauty of language, and at the same time of exactness in correspondence. . . .

The subjects of the Testaments, Old and New, are taken from very primitive and inartificial life. With the exception of the writings of Paul, and in a less degree of Luke, there is little evidence of literary culture or of a wide and varied range of thought in their authors. They narrate plain facts, and they promulgate doctrines, profound indeed, but addressed less to the speculative and discursive than to the moral and spiritual faculties, and hence, whatever may have been the capabilities of Hebrew and of classical Greek for other purposes, the vocabulary of the whole Bible is narrow in extent, and extremely simple in character. Now in the early part of the sixteenth century, when the development of our religious dialect was completed, the English mind and the English language were generally in a state of culture much more analogous to that of the people and the tongues of Palestine, than they have been at any subsequent period. Two centuries later, the native speech had been greatly subtilized, if not refined. Good vernacular words had been supplanted by foreign intruders, comprehensive ideas and their vocabulary had been split up into artificially discriminated thoughts and a corresponding multitude and variety of terms. The language in fact had become too copious and too specific to have any true correspondences with so simple and inartificial a diction as that of the Christian Scriptures. Had the Bible then for the first time appeared in an English dress, the translators would have been perplexed and confounded with the multitude of terms, each expressing a fragment, few the whole, of the meaning of the original words for which they must stand; and whereas three hundred years ago but one good translation was possible, the eighteenth century might have produced a dozen, none altogether good, but none much worse than another. . . .

The critical study of English has but just commenced. We are at the beginning of a new era in its history. Great as are its powers, men are beginning to feel that its necessities are still greater. There is among its authors an evident stretching out for additional facilities of expression, and as a means to this end a deeper reaching down into the wells of its latent capabilities, and hence, as I have so often remarked, a more general and zealous study of those ancient forms of English, out of which was built up the consecrated dialect of our mother tongue.

4. Rhetorical Features of Biblical Language.

[SOUTH, *Christ's Promise the Support of his Despised Ministers.*]

For the ability of speaking conferred upon the apostles. It was highly requisite that those who were to be the interpreters and spokesmen of heaven should have a rhetoric taught them from thence too, and as much beyond any that could be taught them by human rules and art as the subjects they were to speak of surpassed the subject of all human eloquence.

Now this ability of speech, I conceive, was to be attended with these three properties of it : —

1. Great clearness and perspicuity.
2. An unaffected plainness and simplicity. And,
3. A suitable and becoming zeal or fervor. And,

1. For its perspicuity. Christ and his apostles well knew that the great truth delivered by them would support itself, and that barely to deliver it would be abundantly sufficient to enforce it, nakedness, of all things, being never able to make truth ashamed. There was nothing false, faulty, or suspicious in it, and therefore they were not afraid to venture it in the plainest and most intelligible language. Where, indeed, the thing to be spoken is unwarrantable, and the design of the speaker as bad or worse, there

I confess every word may need a cloak of obscurity both to cover and protect it too; but truth and worth neither need nor affect to keep out of sight, nor the lights of the world to wrap themselves in a cloud. The apostles never taught men to preach or pray in an unknown tongue, nor valued such devotion as had ignorance for its parent. Christ still closed his instructions to his disciples with this question, 'Do ye understand these things?' And we find no parable but the rear of it is brought up with an explication. For even when Christ and his apostles preached the most mysterious truths of religion, yet then, though the thing uttered might non-plus their reason, the way and manner of their uttering it was plain, easy, and familiar, and the hearer never put to study when it was his business only to hear and understand. The oracles of Christ were not like those of Apollo, doubtful and ambiguous, always made to deceive, and commonly to destroy; but, on the contrary, as the grand business of our Saviour and his apostles after him was to teach, and that chiefly in order to persuade, so they well knew that there could be no effectual passage into the will but through the judgment, nor any free admission into the former but by a full passport from the latter. And therefore we find not that in their sermons they were for amusing or astonishing their auditory with difficult nothings, rabbinical whimseys, and remote allusions, which no man of sense and solid reason can hear without weariness and contempt.

Besides that, if we look into the reason of the thing itself, it will be found that all obscurity of speech is resolvable into the confusion and disorder of the speaker's thoughts: for as thoughts are properly the images and representations of objects to the mind, and words the representations of our thoughts to others, it must needs follow that all faults or defects in a man's expressions must presuppose the same in his notions first.

In short, nothing in nature can be imagined more absurd, irrational, and contrary to the very design and end of speaking, than an obscure discourse; for in that case the preacher may as well leave his tongue, and his auditors their ears behind them, as neither he communicate, nor they understand, any more of his mind and meaning, after he has spoken to them, than they did before.

And yet, as ridiculous as such fustian bombast from the pulpit is, none are so transported and pleased with it as those who least understand it. For still the greatest admirers of it are the grossest, the most ignorant and illiterate country people, who of all men are the fondest of high-flown metaphors and allegories, attended and set off with scraps of Greek and Latin, though not able even to read so much of the latter as might save their necks upon occasion.

But laying aside all such studied, insignificant trifles, it was the clearness of the apostles' preaching which rendered it victorious and irresistible. And this we may rest upon as certain, that he is still the powerfullest preacher and the best orator who can make himself best understood. But,

2. A second property of the ability of speech conferred by Christ upon his apostles was its unaffected plainness and simplicity; it was to be easy, obvious, and familiar; with nothing in it strained or far-fetched; no affected scheme, or airy fancies, above the reach or relish of an ordinary apprehension; no, nothing of all this; but their grand subject was truth, and consequently above all these petty arts and poor additions, as not being capable of any greater lustre or advantage than to appear just as it is. For there is a certain majesty in plainness; as the proclamation of a prince never frisks it in tropes or fine conceits, in numerous and well-turned periods, but commands in sober, natural expressions. A substantial beauty, as it comes out of the hands of nature, needs neither paint nor patch — things never made to adorn, but to cover something that would be hid. It is with expression, and the clothing of a man's conceptions, as with the clothing of a man's body. All dress and ornament supposes imperfection, as designed only to supply the body with something from without, which it wanted, but had not of its own. Gaudery is a pitiful and a mean thing, not extending further than the surface of the body; nor is the highest gallantry considerable to any, but to those who would hardly be considered without it; for in that case in-

deed there may be great need of an outside, when there is little or nothing within. And thus also it is with the most necessary and important truths; to adorn and clothe them is to cover them, and that to obscure them. . . .

'I speak the words of soberness,' said St. Paul (Acts 26. 25). And I preach the Gospel not with the 'enticing words of man's wisdom' (1 Cor. 2. 4). This was the way of the apostles' discoursing of things sacred. Nothing here of 'the fringes of the North Star'; nothing of 'Nature's becoming unnatural'; nothing of the 'down of angel's wings,' or 'the beautiful locks of cherubims'; no starched similitudes, introduced with a 'Thus have I seen a cloud rolling in its airy mansion,' and the like. No; these were sublimities above the rise of the apostolic spirit. For the apostles, poor mortals, were content to take lower steps, and to tell the world in plain terms that he who believed should be saved, and that he who believed not should be damned. And this was the dialect which pierced the conscience, and made the hearers cry out, 'Men and brethren, what shall we do?' It tickled not the ear, but sunk into the heart; and when men came from such sermons, they never commended the preacher for his taking voice or gesture, for the fineness of such a simile, or the quaintness of such a sentence; but they spoke like men conquered with the overpowering force and evidence of the most concerning truths,— much in the words of the two disciples going to Emmaus, 'Did not our hearts burn within us, while he opened to us the Scriptures?'

In a word, the apostles' preaching was therefore mighty and successful, because plain, natural, and familiar, and by no means above the capacity of their hearers; nothing being more preposterous than for those who were professedly aiming at men's hearts to miss the mark by shooting over their heads.

3. The gift of preaching, conferred by Christ upon his apostles, required a suitable zeal and fervor to attend it; for without this, as high and important a truth as the gospel preached by them was, none would have believed that it had any powerful effect upon the preacher's own affections, nor consequently that it could

have wrought at all more upon other men's; this is most certain. So true is it that the same things, differently expressed, as to the proper effects of persuasion are indeed not the same. A cold indifference dispirits a discourse; but a due fervor gives it life and authority, and sends it home to the inmost powers of the soul, with an easy insinuation and a deep impression. . . .

Thus when Christ accosted Jerusalem with that melting exprobration in Matt. 23. 37, 38, 'O Jerusalem, Jerusalem, thou that killest the prophets, and stonest them that are sent unto thee, how often would I have gathered thy children together, even as a hen gathereth her chickens under her wings, and ye would not! Behold, your house is left unto you desolate.' Now what a relenting strain of tenderness was there in this reproof from the great Doctor as well as Saviour of souls, and how infinitely more moving than if he had said only, 'O ye inhabitants of Jerusalem, how wicked and barbarous is it in you thus to persecute and stone God's prophets! And how can you but expect some severe judgment from God upon you for it?' Who, I say, sees not the vast difference in these two ways of address, as to the vigor and winning compassion of the one, and the low, dispirited flatness of the other in comparison? Likewise for St. Paul, observe how he uttered himself in his excellent farewell discourse to the elders of Ephesus (Acts 20, from verse 18 to the end of the chapter, and particularly in verse 31). 'Remember,' says he, 'how that for the space of three years I ceased not to warn every one night and day with tears.' These were the arguments here used by this great apostle, arguments in comparison of which he knew that the most flowing rhetoric of words would be but a poor and faint persuasive. And then again, in 2 Cor. 11. 29, with what a true and tender passion does he lay forth his fatherly care and concern for all the churches of Christ! 'Who,' says he, 'is weak, and I am not weak? who is offended, and I burn not?' Than which words nothing doubtless could have issued from the tongue or heart of man more endearing, more pathetical and affectionate.

[SOUTH, *The Scribe Instructed.*]

In God's word we have not only a body of religion, but also a system of the best rhetoric; and as the highest things require the highest expressions, so we shall find nothing in Scripture so sublime in itself, but it is reached, and sometimes overtopped, by the sublimity of the expression. And first, where did majesty ever ride in more splendor than in those descriptions of the divine power in Job, in the 38th, 39th, and 40th chapters? And what triumph was ever celebrated with higher, livelier, and more exalted poetry than in the Song of Moses in the 32d of Deuteronomy? And then for the passions of the soul — which being things of the highest transport and most wonderful and various operation in human nature, are therefore the proper object and business of rhetoric — let us take a view how the Scripture expresses the most noted and powerful of them. And here, what poetry ever paralleled Solomon in his description of love, as to all the ways, effects, and ecstasies, and little tyrannies of that commanding passion? See Ovid, with his *Omnia vincit amor*, etc., and Virgil, with his *Vulnus alit venis et cæco carpitur igni*, etc.; how jejune and thin are they to the poetry of Solomon, in the 8th chapter of the Canticles and the 6th verse, 'Love is strong as death, and jealousy cruel as the grave!' And as for his description of beauty, he describes that so, that he even transcribes it into his expressions. And where do we read such strange risings and fallings, now the faintings and languishings, now the terrors and astonishments of despair, venting themselves in such high, amazing strains as in the 77th Psalm? Or where did we ever find sorrow flowing forth in such a natural, prevailing pathos, as in the Lamentations of Jeremy? One would think that every letter was wrote with a tear, every word was the noise of a breaking heart; that the author was a man compacted of sorrows, disciplined to grief from his infancy, one who never breathed but in sighs, nor spoke but in a groan. So that he who said he would not read the Scripture for fear of spoiling his style showed himself as much a blockhead as an atheist, and to have as small a gust of the elegancies of expression as of the sacredness of the matter. And shall we now think that the Scripture forbids all ornament of speech, and engages men to be dull, flat, and slovenly in all their discourses? But let us look a little further, and see whether the New Testament abrogates what we see so frequently used in the Old. And for this, what mean all the parables used by our Saviour, the known and greatest elegancies of speech? So that if this way was unlawful before, Christ by his example has authorized and sanctified it since; and if good and lawful, has confirmed it.

[CARDINAL NEWMAN, *Idea of a University*, pp. 289-290.]

Scripture not elaborate! Scripture not ornamented in diction, and musical in cadence! Why, consider the Epistle to the Hebrews — where is there in the classics any composition more carefully, more artificially written? Consider the book of Job — is it not a sacred drama, as artistic, as perfect, as any Greek tragedy of Sophocles or Euripides? Consider the Psalter — are there no ornaments, no rhythm, no studied cadences, no responsive members, in that divinely beautiful book? And is it not hard to understand? are not the Prophets hard to understand? is not St. Paul hard to understand? Who can say that these are popular compositions? who can say that they are level at first reading with the understandings of the multitude?

That there are portions indeed of the inspired volume more simple both in style and in meaning, and that these are the more sacred and sublime passages, as, for instance, parts of the Gospels, I grant at once; but this does not militate against the doctrine I have been laying down. . . . I have said Literature is one thing, and that Science is another; that Literature has to do with ideas, and Science with realities; that Literature is of a personal character, that Science treats of what is universal and eternal. In proportion, then, as Scripture excludes the personal coloring of its writers, and rises into the region of pure and mere inspiration, when it ceases in any sense to be the writing of man, of St. Paul or St. John, of Moses or Isaias, then it comes to belong to Science, not Literature. Then it conveys the things of heaven, unseen verities, divine manifestations, and them alone — not the ideas, the feelings, the aspirations, of its human instruments, who, for all that they were inspired and infallible, did not cease to be men. St. Paul's epistles, then, I consider to be literature in a real and true sense, *as* personal, *as* rich in reflection and emotion, as Demosthenes or Euripides; and, without ceasing to be revelations of objective truth, they are expressions of the subjective notwithstanding. On the other hand, portions of the Gospels, of the book of Genesis, and other passages of the Sacred Volume, are of the nature of Science. Such is the beginning of St. John's Gospel. . . . Such is the Creed. I mean, passages such as these are the mere enunciation of eternal things, without (so to say) the medium of any human mind transmitting them to us. The words used have the grandeur, the majesty, the calm unimpassioned beauty of Science; they are in no sense Literature, they are in no sense personal; and therefore they are easy to apprehend, and easy to translate.

5. Rhythm of the Bible.

[WATTS, in *Encyclopædia Britannica*, ninth edition, Article *Poetry*.]

Perhaps it may be said that deeper than all the rhythms of art is that rhythm which art would fain catch, the rhythm of nature; for the rhythm of nature is the rhythm of life itself. This rhythm can be caught by prose as well as by poetry, such prose, for instance, as that of the English Bible. Certainly the rhythm of verse at its highest, such, for instance, as that of Shakespeare's greatest writings, is nothing more and nothing less than the metre of that energy of the spirit which surges within the bosom of him who speaks, whether he speak in verse or in impassioned prose. Being rhythm, it is of course governed by law, but it is a law which transcends in subtlety the conscious art of the metricist, and is only caught by the poet in his most inspired moods, a law which, being part of nature's own sanctions, can of course never be formulated, but only expressed as it is expressed in the melody of the bird, in the inscrutable harmony of the entire bird-chorus of a thicket, in the whisper of the leaves of the tree, and in the song or wail of wind and sea. Now is not this rhythm of nature represented by that 'sense rhythm' which prose can catch as well as poetry, that sense rhythm whose finest expressions are to be found in the Bible, Hebrew and English, and in the Biblical movements of the English Prayer Book, and in the dramatic prose of Shakespeare at its best? Whether it is caught by prose or by verse, one of the virtues of the rhythm of nature is that it is translatable. Hamlet's peroration about man and Raleigh's apostrophe to death are as translatable into other languages as are the Hebrew Psalms, or as is Manu's magnificent passage about the singleness of man (we quote from memory) : —

Single is each man born into the world; single he dies; single he receives the reward of his good deeds, and single the punishment of his evil deeds. When he dies his body lies like a fallen tree upon the earth, but his virtue accompanies his soul. Wherefore let man harvest and garner virtue, so that he may have an inseparable companion in traversing that gloom which is so hard to be traversed.

Here the rhythm, being the inevitable movement of emotion and 'sense,' can be caught and translated by every literature under the sun.

[DE MILLE, *Elements of Rhetoric*, § 299.]

The greatest writers of ancient and modern times have sought to infuse into their style something which should appeal to the musical sensibility, and many noble passages in prose literature exert an influence difficult to define, yet so powerful that they affect the heart and cling to the memory. Their meaning is in such cases enlarged and reinforced by the subtle yet potent aid of harmony; and while the thought affects the mind, the music charms the ear. Two things are to be observed in such writings : first, the sound of the individual words; and, secondly, their arrangement, with the recurrence of pauses at such intervals as shall produce a certain harmonious rise and fall of tone. These constitute rhythm in prose.

Many passages in the English Bible exhibit a matchless beauty of rhythm : —

> Or ever the silver cord be loosed — or the golden bowl be broken — or the pitcher be broken at the fountain — or the wheel broken at the cistern. Then shall the dust return to the earth as it was — and the spirit shall return unto God who gave it.
>
> Lord — thou hast been our dwelling-place in all generations.
>
> Before the mountains were brought forth — or ever thou hadst formed the earth and the world — even from everlasting to everlasting — thou art God.
>
> These are they which came out of great tribulation — and have washed their robes — and made them white in the blood of the Lamb.

If these passages be read with attention to the rhetorical pauses, as marked, their euphonious flow and solemn and varied rhythm will not fail to be apparent. It would be difficult to furnish any other translation from their originals which could equal them in this respect.

Rhythm in prose may be defined as the alternate swelling and lessening of sound at certain intervals. It refers to the general effect of sentences and paragraphs, where the words are chosen and arranged so as not only to express the meaning of the writer, but also to furnish a musical accompaniment which shall at once delight the ear by its sound, and help out the sense by its suggestiveness.

[SAINTSBURY, *Specimens of English Prose Style*, Introduction.]

Now the requirement of a perfect prose rhythm is that, while it admits of indication by quantity-marks, and even by divisions into feet, the simplicity and equivalence of feet within the clause answering to the line are absent, and the exact correspondence of clause for clause, that is to say, of line for line, is absent also, and still more necessarily absent. Let us take an example. I know no more perfect example of English prose rhythm than the famous verses of the last chapter of the Canticles in the Authorized Version ; I am not certain that I know any so perfect. Here they are arranged for the purpose of exhibition in clause-lines, quantified and divided into feet.

Sĕt mĕ | ăs ă seāl | ŭpŏn thĭne heārt | ăs ă seāl | ŭpŏn thĭne ārm |
Fŏr lōve | ĭs strōng | ăs deāth | jeālŏusў | ĭs cruĕl | ăs thĕ grāve |
Thĕ coāls thĕrcŏf | āre coāls | ŏf fĭre | which hăth | ă mŏst vē|hĕmĕnt flāme |
Mănў wătĕrs | cănnŏt quĕnch lōve | neīthĕr | căn thĕ floōds | drōwn ĭt |
Ĭf ă măn | should gĭve | ăll thĕ sŭb|stānce | ŏf hĭs hoūse | fŏr lōve | ĭt shoŭld ŭt|tĕrlў bĕ cŏntĕmned. |

I by no means give the quantification of this, or the distribution into lines and feet, as final or impeccable, though I think it is, on the whole — as a good elocutionist would read the passage — accurate enough. But the disposition will, I think, be sufficient to convince any one who has an ear and a slight acquaintance with *res metrica*, that here is a system of rhythm irreducible to poetic form. The movement of the whole is perfectly harmonious, exquisitely modulated, finally complete. But it is the harmony of perfectly modulated speech, not of song; harmony, in short, but not melody, divisible into clauses, but not into bars or staves, having parts which continue each other, but do not correspond to each other. A similar example may be found in the almost equally beautiful Charity passage of the First Epistle to the Corinthians.

[GESENIUS, *Geschichte der hebräischen Sprache und Schrift*, pp. 21–22.]

In particular there exist here two species of diction side by side, the prose of ordinary historical narrative and poetic diction ; the latter, with all its peculiarities, entering likewise into the historical books, the moment prophecies, blessings, or hymns of praise rise to the plane of poetry. This poetical language, clear as such even externally, not, it is true, through prosodic measurement, but rather by the rhythmical marking off of periods, and the parallelism which characterizes them, has likewise many peculiarities in respect to language, verbal forms and meanings, grammatical constructions, etc., — peculiarities which have not always been sufficiently observed. . . . With regard to rhythm and language, the prophets stand midway between poetry and prose; however, those of the golden age closely resemble the poets, and it is only the later ones, like Jeremiah and Ezekiel, who approach the diction of prose.

[DRIVER, *Introduction to the Literature of the Old Testament*, Chap. 7.]

Hebrew Poetry.—Hebrew poetry reaches back to the most ancient recollections of the Israelites (Gen. 49. Nu. 21, 17 f. 27-30. Jud. 5 &c.); probably, as with other nations, it was the form in which their earliest literary efforts found expression. Many poetical pieces are preserved in the historical books; and the Books of Psalms, Proverbs, Job (the Dialogue), Song of Songs, and Lamentations are entirely poetical. The line between poetry and elevated prose being, moreover, less sharply drawn in Hebrew than in Western languages, the prophets not unfrequently rise into a lyric or elegiac strain; and even the author of Ecclesiastes is led sometimes, by the moralizing character of his discourse, to cast his thoughts into the form of gnomic poetry. . . .

Poetry is distinguished from prose partly by the character of the thoughts of which it is the exponent,—which in Hebrew poetry, as a rule, either express or spring out of an emotion,—partly by its diction (the choice and order of words), but especially by its *rhythm*. The onward movement of emotion is not entirely irregular or unrestrained; it is *checked*, or interrupted, at particular intervals; and the flow of thought has to accommodate itself in a certain degree to these recurring interruptions; in other words, it is divided into *lines*. In most Western poetry these lines have a definite *metre* or measure: they consist, viz., of a fixed number of syllables (or of "feet"): in some cases all the lines of a poem being of the same length, in other cases lines of different length alternating, according to certain prescribed rules. To the modern ear, also, the satisfaction which the recurrence of lines of equable length produces, is often enhanced by that assonance of the corresponding lines which we term *rime*. But in ancient Hebrew poetry, though there was always *rhythm*, there was (so far as has yet been discovered) no *metre* in the strict sense of the term; and rime appears to have been as accidental as it was with the classical Latin poets. The poetical instincts of the Hebrews appear to have been satisfied by the adoption of lines of *approximately* the same length, which were combined, as a rule, into groups of two, three, or four lines, constituting *verses*, the verses marking usually more distinct pauses in the progress of the thought than the separate lines. The fundamental (and predominant) form of the Hebrew verse is the couplet of two lines, the second line either repeating, or in some other way reinforcing or completing, the thought of the first. In the verse of two lines is exemplified also the principle which most widely regulates the form of Hebrew poetry, the *parallelismus membrorum* — the parallelism of two clauses of approximately the same length, the second clause answering, or otherwise completing, the thought of the first. The Hebrew verse does not, however, consist uniformly of two lines; the addition of a third line is apt especially to introduce an element of irregularity: so that the *parallelismus membrorum*, though an important canon of Hebrew poetry, is not the *sole* principle by which its form is determined.

The significance in Hebrew poetry of the parallelism of clauses was first perceived by Rob. Lowth, who thus distinguished its principal varieties: —

1. *Synonymous* parallelism. In this kind (which is the most frequent) the second line enforces the thought of the first by repeating, and, as it were, *echoing* it in a varied form, producing an effect at once grateful to the ear and satisfying to the mind: as —

    Nu. 23, 8 How shall I curse, whom God hath not cursed?
        And how shall I defy, whom the LORD hath not defied?

Or the second line expresses a thought not indeed identical with that of the first, but parallel and similar to it —

    Josh. 10, 12 Sun, stand thou still upon Gibeon;
        And thou, Moon, upon the valley of Aijalon.

2. *Antithetic* parallelism. Here the thought of the first line is emphasized, or confirmed, by a *contrasted* thought expressed in the second. Thus —

> Pr. 10, 1 A wise son maketh a glad father,
> But a foolish son is the heaviness of his mother.
> Ps. 1, 6 For the LORD knoweth the way of the righteous;
> But the way of the wicked shall perish.

This kind of parallelism is most frequent in gnomic poetry, where, from the nature of the subject-matter, antithetic truths are often contrasted.

3. *Synthetic* or *constructive* parallelism. Here the second line contains neither a repetition nor a contrast to the thought of the first, but in different ways supplements or completes it. The parallelism, therefore, is merely of *form*, and does not extend to the thought at all. *E.g.* —

> Ps. 2, 6 Yet I have set my king
> Upon Zion, my holy hill.
> Pr. 15, 17 Better is a dinner of herbs where love is,
> Than a stalled ox and hatred therewith.
> 26, 4 Answer not a fool according to his folly,
> Lest thou also be like unto him.
> 27, 8 As a bird that wandereth from her nest,
> So is the man that wandereth from his place.

A comparison, a reason, a consequence, a motive, often constitutes one of the lines in a synthetic parallelism.

4. A fourth kind of parallelism, though of rare occurrence, is still sufficiently marked to be noticed by the side of those described by Lowth, viz. *climactic* parallelism (sometimes called "ascending rhythm"). Here the first line is itself incomplete, and the second line takes up words from it and completes them: —

> Ps. 29, 1 Give unto the LORD, O ye sons of the mighty,
> Give unto the LORD *glory and strength*.
> 8 The voice of the LORD shaketh the wilderness;
> The LORD shaketh the wilderness *of Kadesh*.
> Ex. 15, 16ᵇ Till thy people pass over, O LORD,
> Till the people pass over, *which thou hast purchased*. . . .

By far the greater number of verses in the poetry of the OT. consist of distichs of one or other of the types that have been illustrated; though naturally every individual line is not constructed with the regularity of the examples selected (which, indeed, especially in a long poem, would tend to monotony). The following are the other principal forms of the Hebrew verse: —

1. Single lines, or *monostichs*. These are found but rarely, being generally used to express a thought with some emphasis at the beginning, or occasionally at the end, of a poem: Ps. 16, 1. 18, 1. 23, 1. 66, 1; Ex. 15, 18.

2. Verses of three lines, or *tristichs*. Here different types arise, according to the relation in which the several lines stand to one another. Sometimes, for instance, the three lines are synonymous, as —

> Ps. 5, 11 But let all those that put their trust in thee rejoice,
> Let them ever shout for joy, because thou defendest them:
> And let them that love thy name be joyful in thee.

Sometimes a and b are parallel in thought, and c completes it —

> Ps. 2, 2 The kings of the earth set themselves,
> And the rulers take council together,
> Against Jehovah, and against his anointed.

Or b and c are parallel —

> Ps. 3, 7 Arise, Jehovah; save me, O my God:
> For thou hast smitten all mine enemies upon the cheek-bone;
> Thou hast broken the teeth of the wicked.

Or a and c may be parallel, and b be of the nature of a parenthesis —

> Ps. 4, 2 Answer me, when I call, O God of my righteousness;
> Thou hast set me at large when I was in distress:
> Have mercy upon me, and hear my prayer.

3. *Tetrastichs*. Here generally a is parallel to b, and c is parallel to d; but the thought is only complete when the two couplets are combined; thus —

> Gen. 49, 7 Cursed be their anger, for it was fierce;
> And their wrath, for it was cruel:
> I will divide them in Jacob,
> And scatter them in Israel.

So Dt. 32, 21. 30. 38. 41. Is. 49, 4. 59, 3. 4 &c.
Sometimes, however, a is parallel to c, and b to d —

> Ps. 55, 21 His mouth was smooth as butter,
> But his heart was war;
> His words were softer than oil,
> Yet were they drawn swords.

So Ps. 40, 14. 127, 1. Dt. 32, 42. Is. 30, 16. 44, 5. 49, 2.

Occasionally *a* corresponds to *d*, and *b* to *c*; this is called technically "*introverted* parallelism," but is of rare occurrence; see Pr. 23, 15 f. Is. 11, 13 (Cheyne), 59, 8.

Or *a*, *b*, *c* are parallel, but *d* is more or less independent—

> Ps. 1, 3 And he is as a tree planted by streams of water,
> That bringeth forth its fruit in its season,
> And whose leaf doth not wither:
> And whatsoever he doeth he maketh to prosper.

Or *a* is independent, and *b*, *c*, *d* are parallel—

> Pr. 24, 12 If thou sayest, Behold, we knew not this;
> Doth not he that weigheth the hearts consider it?
> And he that keepeth thy soul, doth not he know it?
> And shall not he render to every man according to his work?

Or it may even happen that the four members stand in no determinate relation to one another; see *e.g.* Ps. 40, 17.

4. and 5. Verses of five lines (*pentastichs*) occur but seldom in the OT., and those of six lines (*hexastichs*) are still rarer; see for the former, Nu. 24, 8. Dt. 32, 14. 39. 1 Sa. 2, 10. Ps. 39, 12. Cant. 3, 4; for the latter, Nu. 24, 17. 1 Sa. 2, 8. Cant. 4, 8. Hab. 3, 17 (three distichs, closely united).

The finest and most perfect specimens of Hebrew poetry are, as a rule, those in which the parallelism is most complete (synonymous distichs and tetrastichs), varied by an occasional tristich (*e.g.* Job 28. 29–31. 38–39. Ps. 18. 29. 104. Pr. 8, 12 ff.; and in a quieter strain, Ps. 51. 81. 91. 103 &c.). . . .

The prophets, though their diction is usually an elevated prose, manifest a strong tendency to enforce and emphasize their thought by casting it, more or less completely, into the form of parallel clauses (*e.g.* Is. 1, 2. 3. 10. 18. 19. 20. 27. 29 &c.; 13, 10. 11. 12. 13 &c.; Am. 6, 1. 2. 3. 4. 5. 6. 7 &c.). And sometimes they adopt a distinctly lyrical strain, as Is. 42, 10–12. 44, 23. 45, 8. But with the prophets the lines are very commonly longer than is the case in poetry (in the technical sense of the word); and the movement is less bright and rapid than that of the true lyrical style.

6. Biblical Style and Language Contrasted with those of Western Nations.

[ADDISON, *Spectator*, No. 405.]

There is a certain coldness and indifference in the phrases of our European languages when they are compared with the Oriental forms of speech; and it happens very luckily that the Hebrew idioms run into the English tongue with a particular grace and beauty. Our language has received innumerable elegancies and improvements from that infusion of Hebraisms which are derived to it out of the poetical passages in Holy Writ. They give a force and energy to our expressions, warm and animate our language, and convey our thoughts in more ardent and intense phrases than any that are to be met with in our own tongue. There is something so pathetic in this kind of diction that it often sets the mind in a flame, and makes our hearts burn within us. . . . If any one would judge of the beauties of poetry that are to be met with in the Divine writings, and examine how kindly the Hebrew manners of speech mix and incorporate with the English language, after having perused the Book of Psalms let him read a literal translation of Horace or Pindar. He will find in these two last such an absurdity and confusion of style, with such a comparative poverty of imagination, as will make him very sensible of what I have been here advancing.

[STEDMAN, *The Nature and Elements of Poetry*, in the *Century Magazine* for May, 1892.]

The naïveté of the Davidic lyre is beyond question, and so is the superb unrestraint of the Hebrew prophecy and pæans. We feel the stress of human nature in its articulate moods. This gives to the poetry of the Scriptures an attribute possessed only by the most creative and impersonal literature of other tongues — that of universality. Again, it was all designed for music, by the poets of a musical race, and the psalms were arranged by the first composers — the leaders of the royal choir. It retains forever the fresh tone of an epoch when lyrical composition was the normal form of expression. Then its rhythm is free, unrestrained, in extreme opposition to that of classical and modern verse, relying merely upon antiphony, alliteration, and parallelism. Technical abandon, allied with directness of conception and faithful revelation of human life, makes for universality — makes of the Hebrew Scriptures a Bible, a world's book that can be translated into all tongues with surpassing effect, notably into a language almost as direct and elemental as its own, that of our Anglo-Saxon in its Jacobean strength and clarity. . . .

It has been said of the Hebrew language that every word is a poem; and there are books of the Old Testament, neither lyrical nor prophetic, so exquisite in kind that I call them models of impersonal art. Considered thus, the purely narrative idyls of Esther and Ruth have so much significance that I shall have occasion to recur to them with reference to poetic beauty and construction.

[CHATEAUBRIAND, *Genius of Christianity*, Part II., Bk. 5, Chaps. 3 and 4.]

So much has been written on the Bible, it has been so repeatedly commented upon, that perhaps the only method now left to make its beauties felt is to compare it with the works of Homer. Consecrated by ages, these poems have received from time a species of sanctity which justifies the parallel and obviates every idea of profanation. If Jacob and Nestor are not of the same family, both at least belong to the early ages of the world, and you feel that it is but a step from the palace of Pylos to the tents of Ishmael.

In what respect the Bible is more beautiful than Homer, what resemblances and what differences exist between it and the productions of that poet — such are the subjects which we purpose to examine in these chapters. Let us consider these two monuments, which stand like solitary columns at the entrance to the temple of Genius, and form its simple peristyle.

In the first place, it is a curious spectacle to behold the rivalry of the two most ancient languages of the world, the languages in which Moses and Lycurgus published their laws, and David and Pindar chanted their hymns. The Hebrew, concise, energetic, with scarcely any inflection in its verbs, expressing twenty shades of a thought by the mere apposition of a letter, proclaims the idiom of a people who, by a remarkable combination, unite primitive simplicity with a profound knowledge of mankind. The Greek . . . displays in its intricate conjugations, in its inflections, in its diffuse eloquence, a nation of an imitative and social genius, a nation elegant and vain, fond of melody and prodigal of words. . . .

Our terms of comparison will be: Simplicity; Antiquity of Manners; Narrative; Description; Similes or Images; the Sublime. Let us examine the first of these terms.

1. *Simplicity.*

The simplicity of the Bible is more concise and more solemn, the simplicity of Homer more diffuse and more lively. The former is sententious, and comes back to the same locutions to express new ideas; the latter is fond of expatiating, and often repeats in the same phrases what has been said before. The simplicity of Scripture is that of an ancient priest, who, imbued with all the sciences, human and divine, pronounces from the recess of the sanctuary the precise oracles of wisdom; the simplicity of the poet of Chios is that of an aged traveler, who, beside the hearth of his host, relates what he has learned in the course of a long and checkered life. . . .

3. *Narrative.*

The narrative of Homer is interrupted by digressions, harangues, descriptions of vessels, garments, arms, and sceptres, by genealogies of men and things. Proper names are always surcharged with epithets; a hero seldom fails to be *divine, like the immortals,* or *honored by the nations as a god.* A princess is sure to have *white arms,* her shape always resembles *the trunk of the palm-tree of Delos,* and she owes her locks to *the youngest of the Graces.*

The narrative of the Bible is rapid, without digression, without circumlocution; it is broken into short sentences, and the persons are named without flattery. Proper names are incessantly recurring, and the pronoun is scarcely ever used instead of them, a circumstance which, added to the frequent repetition of the conjunction *and*, indicates by this simplicity a society much nearer the state of nature than that sung by Homer. The forms of self-love are already evoked in the characters of the Odyssey, whereas they are dormant in those of Genesis.

4. *Description.*

The descriptions of Homer are prolix, whether they be of a pathetic or a terrible character, melancholy or cheerful, energetic or sublime. The Bible, in all its different species of description, gives in general but one single trait, but this trait is striking, and distinctly exhibits the object to our view.

5. *Similes.*

The Homeric similes are lengthened out by accidental circumstances; they are little pictures hung round an edifice to refresh the eye which has been fatigued with the height of the domes, by calling it back to rest on scenes of nature and rural manners. The comparisons of the Bible are almost all given in but few words: you have a lion, a stream, a storm, a fire, roaring, falling, ravaging, devouring. It is, however, no stranger to circumstantial similes, but then it adopts an Oriental turn and personifies the object, as pride in the cedar, etc.

6. *The Sublime.*

Finally, the sublime in Homer commonly arises from the general combination of the parts, and arrives by degrees at its acme. In the Bible it is almost always unexpected; it bursts upon you like lightning, and you are left smoking and riven by the thunderbolt before you know how you were struck by it. In Homer, again, the sublime consists in the magnificence of the words harmonizing with the majesty of the thought. In the Bible, on the contrary, the highest degree of sublimity often proceeds from a contrast between the grandeur of the idea and the littleness, at times even the triviality, of the word that expresses it. From this results a shock, a violent wrench to the mind; for when, raised by contemplation, the soul darts towards the highest regions, suddenly the expression, instead of buoying it up, lets it fall from heaven to earth, and hurls it from the bosom of God to the mire of this nether world. This species of sublime, the most impetuous of all, is admirably adapted to an immense and awful being, allied at once to the greatest and the smallest objects. . . .

We shall conclude this parallel, and the whole subject of Christian poetics, with an essay which will show at once the difference between the style of the Bible and that of Homer; we shall take a passage from the former and paint it with colors borrowed from the latter. Ruth thus addresses Naomi:

"Intreat me not to leave thee, or to return from following after thee; for whither thou goest, I will go; and where thou lodgest I will lodge; thy people shall be my people, and thy God my God; where thou diest will I die, and there will I be buried."

Let us try to render this verse into the language of Homer:

"The fair Ruth thus responds to the wise Naomi, honored by the people as a goddess: 'Cease to oppose the determination with which a divinity inspires me; I will tell thee the truth, just as it is, and without disguise. I am resolved to follow thee. I will remain with thee, whether thou shalt continue to reside among the Moabites, so dexterous in throwing the javelin, or shalt return to Judea, so fertile in olives. With thee I will demand hospitality of the nations who respect the suppliant. Our ashes shall be mingled in the same urn, and I will offer agreeable sacrifices to the God who incessantly accompanies thee.' She said; and as when the vehement West Wind brings a warm, refreshing rain, the husbandmen prepare the wheat and the barley, and make baskets of rushes nicely interwoven, for they foresee that the falling shower will soften the soil and render it fit for receiving the precious gifts of Ceres; so the words of Ruth, like a fertilizing rain, melted the heart of Naomi."

Such, perhaps, as closely as our feeble talents allow us to imitate Homer, is a shadow of the style of that immortal genius. But has not the verse of Ruth, thus amplified, lost the original charm which it possesses in the Scriptures? What poetry can ever be equivalent to this single stroke of eloquence, 'Thy people shall be my people, and thy God my God'?

[RENAN, *Histoire Générale des Langues Sémitiques*, second edition, pp. 18-24.]

The unity and simplicity which distinguish the Semitic race are likewise found in the Semitic languages. Abstraction is unknown to them; metaphysics, impossible. Language being the necessary mold of a people's intellectual operations, an idiom almost destitute of syntax, without variety of construction, lacking the conjunctions which establish such delicate relations among the members of thought, portraying every object by its external qualities, ought to be eminently suitable to the eloquent inspirations of seers and the delineation of fugitive impressions, but should deny itself to all philosophy, to all purely intellectual speculations. To imagine an Aristotle or a Kant with such an organ of expression is as impossible as to conceive an Iliad or a poem like that of Job written in our metaphysical and complicated languages. Add to this that the Semitic languages, especially the older ones, are inexact, and correspond but approximately with the things themselves. Their formulas have not the precision which with us leaves no room for ambiguity. When we seek to translate into our European tongues, where each word has only a single meaning, the oldest monuments of Hebrew poetry, we experience the necessity of putting questions to ourselves, and of making a multitude of distinctions which never occurred to the author, but to which the mechanism of our idioms obliges us to attend.

This physical and sensuous character seems to us the dominant trait of the family of languages which forms the object of our study. Their roots are almost all derived from the imitation of nature, and allow us to perceive, as through transparent crystal, the impressions which, reflected by the consciousness of primitive man, resulted in language. Derivative words are formed according to simple and uniform laws. The verb has a still evident character of priority. . . . The noun has but few inflections. . . . Certain parasitical monosyllables, which agglutinate at the beginning of words, take the place of terminal inflections. . . . Indeed, the whole construction of the sentence displays such a character of simplicity, especially in narrative, that we can only think of the artless stories of a child. Instead of the skilful involutions of phrase (*circuitus, comprehensio,* as Cicero calls them) within whose compass Greek and Latin unite with so much art the various members of a single thought, the Semites can only attach one proposition to the end of another, using as their sole contrivance the simple copula *and,* which serves them in lieu of almost every other conjunction.

Ewald has rightly observed that the language of the Semites is rather poetic and lyrical than oratorical or epic. It is true that the art of oratory, in the classical sense, has always been foreign to them. Semitic grammar is almost ignorant of the art of subordinating the clauses of the sentence; it taxes the race which created it with a patent inferiority of the reasoning faculties, but allows it a very lively sense of reality and much delicacy of sensation. Perspective is wholly wanting to the Semitic style; in vain should we seek in it those sallies, those retreats, those half-lights, which give the Aryan languages a second power of expression, as it were. Plain and destitute of inversions, the Semitic languages are acquainted with no process save the juxtaposition of ideas, after the manner of Byzantine painting or the bas-reliefs of Nineveh. We must even admit that the idea of *style,* as we understand the word, is entirely wanting to the Semites. Their periods are very short; the extent of discourse which they can embrace at once does not exceed one or two lines. Solely concerned with the thought of the moment, they do not prepare in advance the mechanism of the sentence, and never consider what precedes or what is to come. Hence result strange inadvertences, into which they are led by their inability to follow to the end a single idea, and by their practice of never returning to correct what has once been written. It is like the most careless conversation, caught in the act and immediately fixed by writing.

In the structure of the sentence, as in their whole mental constitution, there is with the Semites one intricacy less than with the Aryans. They are destitute of one of the degrees of combination which we esteem necessary for the complete expression of thought. The uniting of words into a proposition is their supreme effort; it never occurs to them to repeat the process on the propositions themselves. This is, according to the expression of Aristotle,[1] the 'indefinite style,' advancing by accumulated atoms, as opposed to the finished rotundity of the Greek and Latin period. Everything which may be included under the denomination of oratorical harmony remained unknown to them. Eloquence is for them only a lively succession of earnest observations and bold images; in rhetoric no less than in architecture their favorite device is the arabesque.

The importance of the verse in Semitic style is the best proof of the total lack of internal construction which characterizes their diction. The verse has nothing in common with the Greek and Latin period, since it does not present a succession of members dependent upon one another; it is an almost arbitrary division in a series of propositions separated by commas. Its length is not determined by anything essential; the verse corresponds to the pauses demanded by the exigencies of respiration, whether or not such pauses are required by the sense. The author stops, not from the feeling that he has arrived at a natural halting-place in his discourse, but simply because he cannot help himself. Let any one attempt to divide up in this way a speech of Demosthenes or Cicero, and he will realize how fully the verse belongs to the very essence of the Semitic languages. It is only at a comparatively recent period that they gave up this feature, an insufficient provision against the wearisome monotony to which they were condemned by their too simple idea of discourse.

We may say that the Aryan tongues, compared with the Semitic,

[1] See p. lxviii.

are the languages of abstraction and metaphysics, compared with those of realism and sensuousness. With their marvelous flexibility, their variety of inflections, their delicate particles, their compound words, and especially because of the admirable secret of inversion, which allows the natural order of ideas to be changed without injury to the determination of grammatical relations, the Aryan languages lead us directly into complete idealism, and induce us to regard the creation of language as a fact essentially transcendental.

If, on the other hand, we considered only the Semitic languages, we might be tempted to believe that sensation alone presided at the first movements of human thought, and that language was in the beginning only a kind of reflex of the external world. In running over the list of Semitic roots, we scarcely encounter a single one which does not offer a primary material sense, applied, by transitions more or less direct, to intellectual objects. Is it a feeling of the soul which is to be expressed, recourse is had to the organic movement which is usually its sign. Thus anger is expressed in Hebrew in a multitude of ways, all alike picturesque, and all derived from physiological circumstances. Now the metaphor is taken from the rapid and animated breathing which accompanies passion[1]; now from heat, or from ebullition; now from the action of breaking with a crash; now from shuddering. Dejection and despair are expressed in this language by internal liquefaction, the dissolution of the heart; fear, by the loosing of the reins. Pride is depicted by the elevation of the head, a tall and erect stature. Patience is a long breathing, impatience a short. Desire is thirst or paleness. Pardon is expressed by a host of metaphors borrowed from the idea of covering, concealing, passing over a sin a coating which blots it out. In the Book of Job, God sews up sins in a bag, affixes his seal, then casts it behind his back, and all this to signify *forgetting*. To shake the head, look upon one another, let fall one's arms, are expressions which Hebrew much prefers to all our psychological terms for the rendering of disdain, indecision, and despondency. We may even say that

---

[1] The Hebrew roots, adduced by the author, are here omitted. — ED.

such psychological terms are almost totally wanting in Hebrew, or at least that there is always added the portrayal of the attendant physical circumstance : ' He grew angry, and his countenance was inflamed . . .; he opened his mouth, and said,' etc.

Other notions more or less abstract have received their symbol, in the Semitic languages, in a like manner. The idea of the true is drawn from solidity, stability; that of the beautiful, from radiance; that of good, from rectitude; that of evil, from deviation, from the curve, or else from stench. To make or create was originally to carve out; to decide anything is to cut across; to think is to speak. ' Bone ' signifies the substance, the inmost of a thing, and serves in Hebrew as the equivalent of the pronoun 'self.' I am not ignorant that similar facts occur in all languages, and that Aryan idioms would furnish almost as many examples where pure thought is, in the same way, involved in a concrete and sensible form. But what distinguishes the Semitic family is that the original fusion of sensation and idea has always been maintained, that neither of the two has thrown the other into the shade, as has come to pass in the Aryan languages; in short, that idealization has never taken place with any thoroughness, so that in every word we imagine we hear the echo of the primitive sensations which determined the choice of those who first bestowed the names.

[ARISTOTLE, *Rhetoric*, Bk. 3, Chap. 9, Welldon's translation.]

By a jointed style I mean one which has no end in itself except the completion of the subject under discussion. It is disagreeable from its endlessness or indefiniteness, as everybody likes to have the end clearly in view. This is the reason why people in a race do not gasp and faint until they reach the goal; for while they have the finishing-point before their eyes, they are insensible of fatigue. The compact style, on the other hand, is the periodic; and I mean by a period a sentence having a beginning and an end in itself, and a magnitude which admits of being easily comprehended at a glance. Such a style is agreeable and can be easily learnt. It is agreeable, as being the opposite of the indefinite style, and because the hearer is constantly imagining himself to have got hold of something, from constantly finding a definite conclusion of the sentence, whereas in the other style there is something disagreeable in having nothing to look forward to or accomplish. It is easily learnt too, as being easily recollected, and this because a periodic style can be numbered, and number is the easiest thing in the world to recollect. It is thus that everybody recollects verses better than irregular or prose compositions, as they contain number and are measured by it. But the period should be completed by the sense as well as by the rhythm, and not be abruptly broken off.

[RENAN, *Histoire Générale des Langues Sémitiques*, pp. 411–413, 418.]

One of the laws most generally observed in the different families of languages, especially the Aryan, is that which refers synthesis and complexity to the beginning. Far from representing the present state as the development of a primitive germ less complete and simple than the state which has succeeded, the most profound linguists are unanimous in placing at the infancy of the human spirit the languages which are synthetic, obscure, and complicated, — so complicated, indeed, that it is the want of an easier language which has led later generations to abandon the learned tongue of their ancestors. It would be possible, by taking one after another the languages of almost all the countries where mankind has had a history, to verify this regular progress from synthesis to analysis. Everywhere an ancient language has made way for a popular speech, which does not constitute, it is true, a new idiom, but is rather a transformation of that which preceded it. The latter was more learned, laden with inflections to express the infinitely delicate relations of thought, even richer in the order of its ideas, though this order was comparatively restricted, — an image, in a word, of primitive spontaneity, in which the mind gathered elements into a confused unity, and lost in the whole the analytic view of the parts. The modern dialect, on the other hand, corresponds to a progress of analysis, is clearer and more explicit, separating what the ancients jumbled together, shattering the mechanism of the ancient language in order to bestow on each idea and relation its own isolated expression. . . . The axiom which we have just enounced is subject to weighty exceptions, recognized by the very persons who formulated it. Friedrich Schlegel dares not apply it to certain languages which have remained in an inferior stage of culture; Abel-Rémusat and Wilhelm von Humboldt have excepted the Chinese language. We believe that in many respects the Semitic languages must share in the same exception. Indeed, so far from complexity being their primitive state, the further we go back toward their origins the more simple they appear; on the contrary, the further we depart from their cradle the fuller and richer they are. . . .

The Semitic languages, considered as a whole, are languages essentially analytical. In place of rendering in its unity the complex element of discourse, they prefer to dissect it, and express it term by term. They are ignorant of the art of establishing among the members of a sentence that reciprocity which makes the period a body whose parts are connected in such a way that the understanding of the one is impossible except through the collective view of the whole. They have not had to shake off the yoke that the comprehensive thought of the fathers of the Aryan race imposed on the spirit of their descendants. The wonderful clearness with which the Semitic race perceived at once the distinction of the *ego*, the world, and God, excluded this vast and simultaneous intuition of relations. The Hebrew sentence is a masterpiece of logical analysis, and we are surprised to find there at every step the explicit turns, the Gallicisms, if I may venture to say so, which seem the heritage of the most positive and reflective tongues.

BIBLICAL SELECTIONS.

Exodus 15.

MOSES' SONG OF DELIVERANCE.

THEN sang Moses and the children of Israel this song unto the LORD, and spake, saying, I will sing unto the LORD, for he hath triumphed gloriously; the horse and his rider hath he thrown into the sea.

2 The LORD is my strength and song, and he is become my salvation; he is my God, and I will prepare him an habitation; my father's God, and I will exalt him.

3 The LORD is a man of war; the LORD is his name.

4 Pharaoh's chariots and his host hath he cast into the sea; his chosen captains also are drowned in the Red sea.

5 The depths have covered them; they sank into the bottom as a stone.

6 Thy right hand, O LORD, is become glorious in power; thy right hand, O LORD, hath dashed in pieces the enemy.

7 And in the greatness of thine excellency thou hast overthrown them that rose up against thee; thou sentest forth thy wrath, which consumed them as stubble.

8 And with the blast of thy nostrils the waters were gathered together, the floods stood upright as an heap, and the depths were congealed in the heart of the sea.

9 The enemy said, I will pursue, I will overtake, I will divide the spoil; my lust shall be satisfied upon them; I will draw my sword, my hand shall destroy them.

10 Thou didst blow with thy wind, the sea covered them; they sank as lead in the mighty waters.

11 Who is like unto thee, O Lord, among the gods? who is like thee, glorious in holiness, fearful in praises, doing wonders?

12 Thou stretchedst out thy right hand,. the earth swallowed them.

13 Thou in thy mercy hast led forth the people which thou hast redeemed; thou hast guided them in thy strength unto thy holy habitation.

14 The people shall hear, and be afraid; sorrow shall take hold on the inhabitants of Palestina.

15 Then the dukes of Edom shall be amazed; the mighty men of Moab, trembling shall take hold upon them; all the inhabitants of Canaan shall melt away.

16 Fear and dread shall fall upon them; by the greatness of thine arm they shall be as still as a stone; till thy people pass over, O Lord, till the people pass over which thou hast purchased.

17 Thou shalt bring them in, and plant them in the mountain of thine inheritance, in the place, O Lord, which thou hast made for thee to dwell in, in the sanctuary, O Lord, which thy hands have established.

18 The Lord shall reign for ever and ever.

19 For the horse of Pharaoh went in with his chariots and with his horsemen into the sea, and the Lord brought again the waters of the sea upon them; but the children of Israel went on dry land in the midst of the sea.

20 And Miriam the prophetess, the sister of Aaron, took a timbrel in her hand; and all the women went out after her with timbrels and with dances.

21 And Miriam answered them, Sing ye to the Lord, for he hath triumphed gloriously; the horse and his rider hath he thrown into the sea.

22 So Moses brought Israel from the Red sea, and they went out into the wilderness of Shur; and they went three days in the wilderness, and found no water.

23 And when they came to Marah, they could not drink of the waters of Marah, for they were bitter; therefore the name of it was called Marah.

24 And the people murmured against Moses, saying, What shall we drink?

25 And he cried unto the LORD; and the LORD showed him a tree, which when he had cast into the waters, the waters were made sweet. There he made for them a statute and an ordinance, and there he proved them,

26 And said, If thou wilt diligently hearken to the voice of the LORD thy God, and wilt do that which is right in his sight, and wilt give ear to his commandments, and keep all his statutes, I will put none of these diseases upon thee, which I have brought upon the Egyptians; for I am the LORD that healeth thee.

27 And they came to Elim, where were twelve wells of water, and threescore and ten palm trees; and they encamped there by the waters.

Exodus 20.

THE LAW GIVEN TO THE CHILDREN OF ISRAEL.

AND God spake all these words, saying,

2 I am the LORD thy God, which have brought thee out of the land of Egypt, out of the house of bondage.

3 Thou shalt have no other gods before me.

4 Thou shalt not make unto thee any graven image, or any likeness of any thing that is in heaven above, or that is in the earth beneath, or that is in the water under the earth;

5 Thou shalt not bow down thyself to them, nor serve them; for I the LORD thy God am a jealous God, visiting the iniquity of the fathers upon the children unto the third and fourth generation of them that hate me,

6 And showing mercy unto thousands of them that love me and keep my commandments.

7 Thou shalt not take the name of the Lord thy God in vain; for the Lord will not hold him guiltless that taketh his name in vain.

8 Remember the sabbath day, to keep it holy.

9 Six days shalt thou labor, and do all thy work;

10 But the seventh day is the sabbath of the Lord thy God; in it thou shalt not do any work, thou, nor thy son, nor thy daughter, thy manservant, nor thy maidservant, nor thy cattle, nor thy stranger that is within thy gates;

11 For in six days the Lord made heaven and earth, the sea, and all that in them is, and rested the seventh day: wherefore the Lord blessed the sabbath day, and hallowed it.

12 Honor thy father and thy mother, that thy days may be long upon the land which the Lord thy God giveth thee.

13 Thou shalt not kill.

14 Thou shalt not commit adultery.

15 Thou shalt not steal.

16 Thou shalt not bear false witness against thy neighbor.

17 Thou shalt not covet thy neighbor's house, thou shalt not covet thy neighbor's wife, nor his manservant, nor his maidservant, nor his ox, nor his ass, nor any thing that is thy neighbor's.

18 And all the people saw the thunderings, and the lightnings, and the noise of the trumpet, and the mountain smoking; and when the people saw it, they removed, and stood afar off.

19 And they said unto Moses, Speak thou with us, and we will hear; but let not God speak with us, lest we die.

20 And Moses said unto the people, Fear not; for God is come to prove you, and that his fear may be before your faces, that ye sin not.

21 And the people stood afar off, and Moses drew near unto the thick darkness where God was.

22 And the Lord said unto Moses, Thus thou shalt say unto the children of Israel, Ye have seen that I have talked with you from heaven.

23 Ye shall not make with me gods of silver, neither shall ye make unto you gods of gold.

24 An altar of earth thou shalt make unto me, and shalt sacrifice thereon thy burnt offerings, and thy peace offerings, thy sheep, and thine oxen; in all places where I record my name I will come unto thee, and I will bless thee.

25 And if thou wilt make me an altar of stone, thou shalt not build it of hewn stone; for if thou lift up thy tool upon it, thou hast polluted it.

26 Neither shalt thou go up by steps unto mine altar, that thy nakedness be not discovered thereon.

Deuteronomy 32.

THE SONG OF MOSES.

GIVE ear, O ye heavens, and I will speak; and hear, O earth, the words of my mouth.

2 My doctrine shall drop as the rain, my speech shall distil as the dew, as the small rain upon the tender herb, and as the showers upon the grass;

3 Because I will publish the name of the LORD; ascribe ye greatness unto our God.

4 He is the Rock, his work is perfect, for all his ways are judgment; a God of truth and without iniquity, just and right is he.

5 They have corrupted themselves, their spot is not the spot of his children; they are a perverse and crooked generation.

6 Do ye thus requite the LORD, O foolish people and unwise? is not he thy father that hath bought thee? hath he not made thee, and established thee?

7 Remember the days of old, consider the years of many generations; ask thy father, and he will show thee, thy elders, and they will tell thee.

8 When the Most High divided to the nations their inheritance, when he separated the sons of Adam, he set the bounds of the people according to the number of the children of Israel.

9 For the Lord's portion is his people; Jacob is the lot of his inheritance.

10 He found him in a desert land, and in the waste howling wilderness; he led him about, he instructed him, he kept him as the apple of his eye.

11 As an eagle stirreth up her nest, fluttereth over her young, spreadeth abroad her wings, taketh them, beareth them on her wings,

12 So the Lord alone did lead him, and there was no strange god with him.

13 He made him ride on the high places of the earth, that he might eat the increase of the fields; and he made him to suck honey out of the rock, and oil out of the flinty rock;

14 Butter of kine, and milk of sheep, with fat of lambs, and rams of the breed of Bashan, and goats, with the fat of kidneys of wheat; and thou didst drink the pure blood of the grape.

15 But Jeshurun waxed fat, and kicked; thou art waxen fat, thou art grown thick, thou art covered with fatness; then he forsook God which made him, and lightly esteemed the Rock of his salvation.

16 They provoked him to jealousy with strange gods, with abominations provoked they him to anger.

17 They sacrificed unto devils, not to God; to gods whom they knew not, to new gods that came newly up, whom your fathers feared not.

18 Of the Rock that begat thee thou art unmindful, and hast forgotten God that formed thee.

19 And when the Lord saw it, he abhorred them, because of the provoking of his sons and of his daughters.

20 And he said, I will hide my face from them, I will see what their end shall be, for they are a very froward generation, children in whom is no faith.

21 They have moved me to jealousy with that which is not God; they have provoked me to anger with their vanities; and I will move them to jealousy with those which are not a people; I will provoke them to anger with a foolish nation.

22 For a fire is kindled in mine anger, and shall burn unto the lowest hell, and shall consume the earth with her increase, and set on fire the foundations of the mountains.

23 I will heap mischiefs upon them; I will spend mine arrows upon them.

24 They shall be burnt with hunger, and devoured with burning heat, and with bitter destruction; I will also send the teeth of beasts upon them, with the poison of serpents of the dust.

25 The sword without, and terror within, shall destroy both the young man and the virgin, the suckling also with the man of gray hairs.

26 I said, I would scatter them into corners, I would make the remembrance of them to cease from among men,

27 Were it not that I feared the wrath of the enemy, lest their adversaries should behave themselves strangely, and lest they should say, Our hand is high, and the LORD hath not done all this.

28 For they are a nation void of counsel, neither is there any understanding in them.

29 O that they were wise, that they understood this, that they would consider their latter end!

30 How should one chase a thousand, and two put ten thousand to flight, except their Rock had sold them, and the LORD had shut them up?

31 For their rock is not as our Rock, even our enemies themselves being judges.

32 For their vine is of the vine of Sodom, and of the fields of Gomorrah; their grapes are grapes of gall, their clusters are bitter;

33 Their wine is the poison of dragons, and the cruel venom of asps.

34 Is not this laid up in store with me, and sealed up among my treasures?

35 To me belongeth vengeance and recompense; their foot shall slide in due time; for the day of their calamity is at hand, and the things that shall come upon them make haste.

36 For the Lord shall judge his people, and repent himself for his servants, when he seeth that their power is gone, and there is none shut up, or left.

37 And he shall say, Where are their gods, their rock in whom they trusted,

38 Which did eat the fat of their sacrifices, and drank the wine of their drink offerings? let them rise up and help you, and be your protection.

39 See now that I, even I, am he, and there is no god with me; I kill, and I make alive; I wound, and I heal; neither is there any that can deliver out of my hand.

40 For I lift up my hand to heaven, and say, I live for ever.

41 If I whet my glittering sword, and mine hand take hold on judgment, I will render vengeance to mine enemies, and will reward them that hate me.

42 I will make mine arrows drunk with blood, and my sword shall devour flesh; and that with the blood of the slain and of the captives, from the beginning of revenges upon the enemy.

43 Rejoice, O ye nations, with his people; for he will avenge the blood of his servants, and will render vengeance to his adversaries, and will be merciful unto his land and to his people.

44 And Moses came and spake all the words of this song in the ears of the people, he, and Hoshea the son of Nun.

45 And Moses made an end of speaking all these words to all Israel;

46 And he said unto them, Set your hearts unto all the words which I testify among you this day, which ye shall command your children to observe to do, all the words of this law.

47 For it is not a vain thing for you; because it is your life, and through this thing ye shall prolong your days in the land, whither ye go over Jordan to possess it.

48 And the Lord spake unto Moses that selfsame day, saying,

49 Get thee up into this mountain Abarim, unto mount Nebo which is in the land of Moab, that is over against Jericho; and behold the land of Canaan, which I give unto the children of Israel for a possession;

50 And die in the mount whither thou goest up, and be gathered unto thy people, as Aaron thy brother died in mount Hor, and was gathered unto his people;

51 Because ye trespassed against me among the children of Israel at the waters of Meribah-Kadesh, in the wilderness of Zin; because ye sanctified me not in the midst of the children of Israel.

52 Yet thou shalt see the land before thee; but thou shalt not go thither unto the land which I give the children of Israel.

2 Samuel 1 : 17–27.

DAVID'S LAMENT OVER SAUL AND JONATHAN.

AND David lamented with this lamentation over Saul and over Jonathan his son:

18 (Also he bade them teach the children of Judah the use of the bow; behold, it is written in the book of Jasher.)

19 The beauty of Israel is slain upon thy high places; how are the mighty fallen!

20 Tell it not in Gath, publish it not in the streets of Askelon; lest the daughters of the Philistines rejoice, lest the daughters of the uncircumcised triumph.

21 Ye mountains of Gilboa, let there be no dew, neither let there be rain, upon you, nor fields of offerings; for there the shield of the mighty is vilely cast away, the shield of Saul, as though he had not been anointed with oil.

22 From the blood of the slain, from the fat of the mighty, the bow of Jonathan turned not back, and the sword of Saul returned not empty.

23 Saul and Jonathan were lovely and pleasant in their lives, and in their death they were not divided; they were swifter than eagles, they were stronger than lions.

24 Ye daughters of Israel, weep over Saul, who clothed you in scarlet, with other delights, who put on ornaments of gold upon your apparel.

25 How are the mighty fallen in the midst of the battle! O Jonathan, thou wast slain in thine high places.

26 I am distressed for thee, my brother Jonathan; very pleasant hast thou been unto me; thy love to me was wonderful, passing the love of women.

27 How are the mighty fallen, and the weapons of war perished!

---

1 Kings 8.

DEDICATION OF THE TEMPLE AND SOLOMON'S PRAYER.

THEN Solomon assembled the elders of Israel, and all the heads of the tribes, the chief of the fathers of the children of Israel, unto king Solomon in Jerusalem, that they might bring up the ark of the covenant of the Lord out of the city of David, which is Zion.

2 And all the men of Israel assembled themselves unto king Solomon at the feast in the month Ethanim, which is the seventh month.

3 And all the elders of Israel came, and the priests took up the ark.

4 And they brought up the ark of the LORD, and the tabernacle of the congregation, and all the holy vessels that were in the tabernacle, even those did the priests and the Levites bring up.

5 And king Solomon, and all the congregation of Israel, that were assembled unto him, were with him before the ark, sacrificing sheep and oxen, that could not be told nor numbered for multitude.

6 And the priests brought in the ark of the covenant of the LORD unto his place, into the oracle of the house, to the most holy place, even under the wings of the cherubims.

7 For the cherubims spread forth their two wings over the place of the ark, and the cherubims covered the ark and the staves thereof above.

8 And they drew out the staves, that the ends of the staves were seen out in the holy place before the oracle, and they were not seen without; and there they are unto this day.

9 There was nothing in the ark save the two tables of stone which Moses put there at Horeb, when the LORD made a covenant with the children of Israel, when they came out of the land of Egypt.

10 And it came to pass, when the priests were come out of the holy place, that the cloud filled the house of the LORD,

11 So that the priests could not stand to minister because of the cloud; for the glory of the LORD had filled the house of the LORD.

12 Then spake Solomon, The LORD said that he would dwell in the thick darkness.

13 I have surely built thee an house to dwell in, a settled place for thee to abide in for ever.

14 And the king turned his face about, and blessed all the congregation of Israel; (and all the congregation of Israel stood;)

15 And he said, Blessed be the LORD God of Israel, which spake with his mouth unto David my father, and hath with his hand fulfilled it, saying,

16 Since the day that I brought forth my people Israel out of Egypt, I chose no city out of all the tribes of Israel to build an house, that my name might be therein; but I chose David to be over my people Israel.

17 And it was in the heart of David my father to build an house for the name of the LORD God of Israel.

18 And the LORD said unto David my father, Whereas it was in thine heart to build an house unto my name, thou didst well that it was in thine heart.

19 Nevertheless thou shalt not build the house; but thy son that shall come forth out of thy loins, he shall build the house unto my name.

20 And the LORD hath performed his word that he spake, and I am risen up in the room of David my father, and sit on the throne of Israel, as the LORD promised, and have built an house for the name of the LORD God of Israel.

21 And I have set there a place for the ark, wherein is the covenant of the LORD, which he made with our fathers, when he brought them out of the land of Egypt.

22 And Solomon stood before the altar of the LORD in the presence of all the congregation of Israel, and spread forth his hands toward heaven;

23 And he said, LORD God of Israel, there is no God like thee, in heaven above, or on earth beneath, who keepest covenant and mercy with thy servants that walk before thee with all their heart;

24 Who hast kept with thy servant David my father that thou promisedst him; thou spakest also with thy mouth, and hast fulfilled it with thine hand, as it is this day.

25 Therefore now, LORD God of Israel, keep with thy servant David my father that thou promisedst him, saying, There shall not fail thee a man in my sight to sit on the throne of Israel; so that thy children take heed to their way, that they walk before me as thou hast walked before me.

26 And now, O God of Israel, let thy word, I pray thee, be verified, which thou spakest unto thy servant David my father.

27 But will God indeed dwell on the earth? behold, the heaven and heaven of heavens cannot contain thee; how much less this house that I have builded?

28 Yet have thou respect unto the prayer of thy servant, and to his supplication, O LORD my God, to hearken unto the cry and to the prayer, which thy servant prayeth before thee to day;

29 That thine eyes may be open toward this house night and day, even toward the place of which thou hast said, My name shall be there; that thou mayest hearken unto the prayer which thy servant shall make toward this place.

30 And hearken thou to the supplication of thy servant, and of thy people Israel, when they shall pray toward this place; and hear thou in heaven thy dwelling place: and when thou hearest, forgive.

31 If any man trespass against his neighbor, and an oath be laid upon him to cause him to swear, and the oath come before thine altar in this house;

32 Then hear thou in heaven, and do, and judge thy servants, condemning the wicked, to bring his way upon his head, and justifying the righteous, to give him according to his righteousness.

33 When thy people Israel be smitten down before the enemy, because they have sinned against thee, and shall turn again to thee, and confess thy name, and pray, and make supplication unto thee in this house ;

34 Then hear thou in heaven, and forgive the sin of thy people Israel, and bring them again unto the land which thou gavest unto their fathers.

35 When heaven is shut up, and there is no rain, because they have sinned against thee ; if they pray toward this place, and confess thy name, and turn from their sin, when thou afflictest them ;

36 Then hear thou in heaven, and forgive the sin of thy servants, and of thy people Israel, that thou teach them the good way wherein they should walk, and give rain upon thy land, which thou hast given to thy people for an inheritance.

37 If there be in the land famine, if there be pestilence, blasting, mildew, locust, or if there be caterpillar ; if their enemy besiege them in the land of their cities ; whatsoever plague, whatsoever sickness there be ;

38 What prayer and supplication soever be made by any man, or by all thy people Israel, which shall know every man the plague of his own heart, and spread forth his hands toward this house ;

39 Then hear thou in heaven thy dwelling place, and forgive, and do, and give to every man according to his ways, whose heart thou knowest ; (for thou, even thou only, knowest the hearts of all the children of men ;)

40 That they may fear thee all the days that they live in the land which thou gavest unto our fathers.

41 Moreover concerning a stranger, that is not of thy people Israel, but cometh out of a far country for thy name's sake ;

42 (For they shall hear of thy great name, and of thy strong hand, and of thy stretched out arm ;) when he shall come and pray toward this house ;

43 Hear thou in heaven thy dwelling place, and do according to

all that the stranger calleth to thee for; that all people of the earth may know thy name, to fear thee, as do thy people Israel; and that they may know that this house, which I have builded, is called by thy name.

44 If thy people go out to battle against their enemy, whithersoever thou shalt send them, and shall pray unto the LORD toward the city which thou hast chosen, and toward the house that I have built for thy name;

45 Then hear thou in heaven their prayer and their supplication, and maintain their cause.

46 If they sin against thee, (for there is no man that sinneth not,) and thou be angry with them, and deliver them to the enemy, so that they carry them away captives unto the land of the enemy, far or near;

47 Yet if they shall bethink themselves in the land whither they were carried captives, and repent, and make supplication unto thee in the land of them that carried them captives, saying, We have sinned, and have done perversely, we have committed wickedness;

48 And so return unto thee with all their heart and with all their soul, in the land of their enemies which led them away captive, and pray unto thee toward their land, which thou gavest unto their fathers, the city which thou hast chosen, and the house which I have built for thy name;

49 Then hear thou their prayer and their supplication in heaven thy dwelling place, and maintain their cause,

50 And forgive thy people that have sinned against thee, and all their transgressions wherein they have transgressed against thee, and give them compassion before them who carried them captive, that they may have compassion on them;

51 For they be thy people, and thine inheritance, which thou broughtest forth out of Egypt, from the midst of the furnace of iron;

52 That thine eyes may be open unto the supplication of thy servant, and unto the supplication of thy people Israel, to hearken unto them in all that they call for unto thee.

53 For thou didst separate them from among all the people of the earth to be thine inheritance, as thou spakest by the hand of Moses thy servant, when thou broughtest our fathers out of Egypt, O Lord God.

54 And it was so, that when Solomon had made an end of praying all this prayer and supplication unto the Lord, he arose from before the altar of the Lord, from kneeling on his knees with his hands spread up to heaven.

55 And he stood, and blessed all the congregation of Israel with a loud voice, saying,

56 Blessed be the Lord, that hath given rest unto his people Israel, according to all that he promised : there hath not failed one word of all his good promise, which he promised by the hand of Moses his servant.

57 The Lord our God be with us, as he was with our fathers; let him not leave us, nor forsake us ;

58 That he may incline our hearts unto him, to walk in all his ways, and to keep his commandments, and his statutes, and his judgments, which he commanded our fathers.

59 And let these my words, wherewith I have made supplication before the Lord, be nigh unto the Lord our God day and night, that he maintain the cause of his servant, and the cause of his people Israel at all times, as the matter shall require ;

60 That all the people of the earth may know that the Lord is God, and that there is none else.

61 Let your heart therefore be perfect with the Lord our God, to walk in his statutes, and to keep his commandments, as at this day.

62 And the king, and all Israel with him, offered sacrifice before the Lord.

63 And Solomon offered a sacrifice of peace offerings, which he offered unto the Lord, two and twenty thousand oxen, and an hundred and twenty thousand sheep. So the king and all the children of Israel dedicated the house of the Lord.

64 The same day did the king hallow the middle of the court that was before the house of the Lord ; for there he offered burnt

offerings, and meat offerings, and the fat of the peace offerings; because the brazen altar that was before the LORD was too little to receive the burnt offerings, and meat offerings, and the fat of the peace offerings.

65 And at that time Solomon held a feast, and all Israel with him, a great congregation, from the entering in of Hamath unto the river of Egypt, before the LORD our God, seven days and seven days, even fourteen days.

66 On the eighth day he sent the people away; and they blessed the king, and went unto their tents joyful and glad of heart for all the goodness that the LORD had done for David his servant, and for Israel his people.

Psalm 23.

THE LORD is my shepherd; I shall not want.
2 He maketh me to lie down in green pastures; he leadeth me beside the still waters.

3 He restoreth my soul; he leadeth me in the paths of righteousness for his name's sake.

4 Yea, though I walk through the valley of the shadow of death, I will fear no evil; for thou art with me; thy rod and thy staff they comfort me.

5 Thou preparest a table before me in the presence of mine enemies; thou anointest my head with oil; my cup runneth over.

6 Surely goodness and mercy shall follow me all the days of my life; and I will dwell in the house of the LORD for ever.

Psalm 32.

BLESSED is he whose transgression is forgiven, whose sin is covered.
2 Blessed is the man unto whom the LORD imputeth not iniquity, and in whose spirit there is no guile.

3 When I kept silence, my bones waxed old through my roaring all the day long.

4 For day and night thy hand was heavy upon me; my moisture is turned into the drought of summer. [Selah.

5 I acknowledged my sin unto thee, and mine iniquity have I not hid. I said, I will confess my transgressions unto the LORD; and thou forgavest the iniquity of my sin. [Selah.

6 For this shall every one that is godly pray unto thee in a time when thou mayest be found; surely in the floods of great waters they shall not come nigh unto him.

7 Thou art my hiding place; thou shalt preserve me from trouble; thou shalt compass me about with songs of deliverance. [Selah.

8 I will instruct thee and teach thee in the way which thou shalt go; I will guide thee with mine eye.

9 Be ye not as the horse, or as the mule, which have no understanding; whose mouth must be held in with bit and bridle, lest they come near unto thee.

10 Many sorrows shall be to the wicked; but he that trusteth in the LORD, mercy shall compass him about.

11 Be glad in the LORD, and rejoice, ye righteous; and shout for joy, all ye that are upright in heart.

Psalm 90.

LORD, thou hast been our dwelling place in all generations.

2 Before the mountains were brought forth, or ever thou hadst formed the earth and the world, even from everlasting to everlasting, thou art God.

3 Thou turnest man to destruction; and sayest, Return, ye children of men.

4 For a thousand years in thy sight are but as yesterday when it is past, and as a watch in the night.

5 Thou carriest them away as with a flood; they are as a sleep; in the morning they are like grass which groweth up.

6 In the morning it flourisheth, and groweth up; in the evening it is cut down, and withereth.

7 For we are consumed by thine anger, and by thy wrath are we troubled.

8 Thou hast set our iniquities before thee, our secret sins in the light of thy countenance.

9 For all our days are passed away in thy wrath; we spend our years as a tale that is told.

10 The days of our years are threescore years and ten; and if by reason of strength they be fourscore years, yet is their strength labor and sorrow; for it is soon cut off, and we fly away.

11 Who knoweth the power of thine anger? even according to thy fear, so is thy wrath.

12 So teach us to number our days, that we may apply our hearts unto wisdom.

13 Return, O LORD, how long! and let it repent thee concerning thy servants.

14 O satisfy us early with thy mercy, that we may rejoice and be glad all our days.

15 Make us glad according to the days wherein thou hast afflicted us, and the years wherein we have seen evil.

16 Let thy work appear unto thy servants, and thy glory unto their children.

17 And let the beauty of the LORD our God be upon us; and establish thou the work of our hands upon us; yea, the work of our hands establish thou it.

Psalm 91.

HE that dwelleth in the secret place of the Most High shall abide under the shadow of the Almighty.

2 I will say of the LORD, He is my refuge and my fortress; my God; in him will I trust.

3 Surely he shall deliver thee from the snare of the fowler, and from the noisome pestilence.

4 He shall cover thee with his feathers, and under his wings shalt thou trust; his truth shall be thy shield and buckler.

5 Thou shalt not be afraid for the terror by night; nor for the arrow that flieth by day;

6 Nor for the pestilence that walketh in darkness; nor for the destruction that wasteth at noonday.

7 A thousand shall fall at thy side, and ten thousand at thy right hand; but it shall not come nigh thee.

8 Only with thine eyes shalt thou behold and see the reward of the wicked.

9 Because thou hast made the LORD, which is my refuge, even the Most High, thy habitation,

10 There shall no evil befall thee, neither shall any plague come nigh thy dwelling.

11 For he shall give his angels charge over thee, to keep thee in all thy ways.

12 They shall bear thee up in their hands, lest thou dash thy foot against a stone.

13 Thou shalt tread upon the lion and adder; the young lion and the dragon shalt thou trample under feet.

14 Because he hath set his love upon me, therefore will I deliver him; I will set him on high, because he hath known my name.

15 He shall call upon me, and I will answer him; I will be with him in trouble; I will deliver him, and honor him.

16 With long life will I satisfy him, and show him my salvation.

Psalm 103.

BLESS the LORD, O my soul; and all that is within me, bless his holy name.

2 Bless the LORD, O my soul, and forget not all his benefits;

3 Who forgiveth all thine iniquities; who healeth all thy diseases;

4 Who redeemeth thy life from destruction; who crowneth thee with lovingkindness and tender mercies;

5 Who satisfieth thy mouth with good things; so that thy youth is renewed like the eagle's.

6 The LORD executeth righteousness and judgment for all that are oppressed.

7 He made known his ways unto Moses, his acts unto the children of Israel.

8 The LORD is merciful and gracious, slow to anger, and plenteous in mercy.

9 He will not always chide; neither will he keep his anger for ever.

10 He hath not dealt with us after our sins; nor rewarded us according to our iniquities.

11 For as the heaven is high above the earth, so great is his mercy toward them that fear him.

12 As far as the east is from the west, so far hath he removed our transgressions from us.

13 Like as a father pitieth his children, so the LORD pitieth them that fear him.

14 For he knoweth our frame; he remembereth that we are dust.

15 As for man, his days are as grass; as a flower of the field, so he flourisheth.

16 For the wind passeth over it, and it is gone; and the place thereof shall know it no more.

17 But the mercy of the LORD is from everlasting to everlasting upon them that fear him, and his righteousness unto children's children,

18 To such as keep his covenant, and to those that remember his commandments to do them.

19 The LORD hath prepared his throne in the heavens; and his kingdom ruleth over all.

20 Bless the LORD, ye his angels, that excel in strength, that do his commandments, hearkening unto the voice of his word.

21 Bless ye the LORD, all ye his hosts; ye ministers of his, that do his pleasure.

22 Bless the LORD, all his works in all places of his dominion; bless the LORD, O my soul.

Psalm 112.

PRAISE ye the LORD. Blessed is the man that feareth the LORD, that delighteth greatly in his commandments.

2 His seed shall be mighty upon earth; the generation of the upright shall be blessed.

3 Wealth and riches shall be in his house; and his righteousness endureth for ever.

4 Unto the upright there ariseth light in the darkness; he is gracious, and full of compassion, and righteous.

5 A good man sheweth favor, and lendeth; he will guide his affairs with discretion.

6 Surely he shall not be moved for ever; the righteous shall be in everlasting remembrance.

7 He shall not be afraid of evil tidings; his heart is fixed, trusting in the LORD.

8 His heart is established, he shall not be afraid, until he see his desire upon his enemies.

9 He hath dispersed, he hath given to the poor; his righteousness endureth for ever; his horn shall be exalted with honor.

10 The wicked shall see it, and be grieved; he shall gnash with his teeth, and melt away; the desire of the wicked shall perish.

Psalm 119.

א (ALEPH).

BLESSED are the undefiled in the way, who walk in the law of the LORD.

2 Blessed are they that keep his testimonies, and that seek him with the whole heart.

3 They also do no iniquity; they walk in his ways.

4 Thou hast commanded us to keep thy precepts diligently.

5 O that my ways were directed to keep thy statutes!

6 Then shall I not be ashamed, when I have respect unto all thy commandments.

7 I will praise thee with uprightness of heart, when I shall have learned thy righteous judgments.

8 I will keep thy statutes; O forsake me not utterly.

ב (BETH).

9 Wherewithal shall a young man cleanse his way? by taking heed thereto according to thy word.

10 With my whole heart have I sought thee; O let me not wander from thy commandments.

11 Thy word have I hid in mine heart, that I might not sin against thee.

12 Blessed art thou, O LORD; teach me thy statutes.

13 With my lips have I declared all the judgments of thy mouth.

14 I have rejoiced in the way of thy testimonies, as much as in all riches.

15 I will meditate in thy precepts, and have respect unto thy ways.

16 I will delight myself in thy statutes; I will not forget thy word.

ג (GIMEL).

17 Deal bountifully with thy servant, that I may live, and keep thy word.

18 Open thou mine eyes, that I may behold wondrous things out of thy law.

19 I am a stranger in the earth; hide not thy commandments from me.

20 My soul breaketh for the longing that it hath unto thy judgments at all times.

21 Thou hast rebuked the proud that are cursed, which do err from thy commandments.

22 Remove from me reproach and contempt; for I have kept thy testimonies.

23 Princes also did sit and speak against me; but thy servant did meditate in thy statutes.

24 Thy testimonies also are my delight and my counsellors.

ד (DALETH).

25 My soul cleaveth unto the dust; quicken thou me according to thy word.

26 I have declared my ways, and thou heardest me; teach me thy statutes.

27 Make me to understand the way of thy precepts; so shall I talk of thy wondrous works.

28 My soul melteth for heaviness; strengthen thou me according unto thy word.

29 Remove from me the way of lying; and grant me thy law graciously.

30 I have chosen the way of truth; thy judgments have I laid before me.

31 I have stuck unto thy testimonies; O LORD, put me not to shame.

32 I will run the way of thy commandments, when thou shalt enlarge my heart.

ה (HE).

33 Teach me, O LORD, the way of thy statutes; and I shall keep it unto the end.

34 Give me understanding, and I shall keep thy law; yea, I shall observe it with my whole heart.

35 Make me to go in the path of thy commandments; for therein do I delight.

36 Incline my heart unto thy testimonies, and not to covetousness.

37 Turn away mine eyes from beholding vanity; and quicken thou me in thy way.

38 Stablish thy word unto thy servant, who is devoted to thy fear.

39 Turn away my reproach which I fear; for thy judgments are good.

40 Behold, I have longed after thy precepts; quicken me in thy righteousness.

ו (VAU).

41 Let thy mercies come also unto me, O LORD, even thy salvation, according to thy word.

42 So shall I have wherewith to answer him that reproacheth me; for I trust in thy word.

43 And take not the word of truth utterly out of my mouth; for I have hoped in thy judgments.

44 So shall I keep thy law continually for ever and ever.

45 And I will walk at liberty; for I seek thy precepts.

46 I will speak of thy testimonies also before kings, and will not be ashamed.

47 And I will delight myself in thy commandments, which I have loved.

48 My hands also will I lift up unto thy commandments, which I have loved; and I will meditate in thy statutes.

ז (ZAIN).

49 Remember the word unto thy servant, upon which thou hast caused me to hope.

50 This is my comfort in my affliction; for thy word hath quickened me.

51 The proud have had me greatly in derision; yet have I not declined from thy law.

52 I remembered thy judgments of old, O LORD; and have comforted myself.

53 Horror hath taken hold upon me because of the wicked that forsake thy law.

54 Thy statutes have been my songs in the house of my pilgrimage.

55 I have remembered thy name, O LORD, in the night, and have kept thy law.

56 This I had, because I kept thy precepts.

ח (CHETH).

57 Thou art my portion, O LORD; I have said that I would keep thy words.

58 I entreated thy favor with my whole heart; be merciful unto me according to thy word.

59 I thought on my ways, and turned my feet unto thy testimonies.

60 I made haste, and delayed not to keep thy commandments.

61 The bands of the wicked have robbed me: but I have not forgotten thy law.

62 At midnight I will rise to give thanks unto thee because of thy righteous judgments.

63 I am a companion of all them that fear thee, and of them that keep thy precepts.

64 The earth, O LORD, is full of thy mercy; teach me thy statutes.

ט (TETH).

65 Thou hast dealt well with thy servant, O LORD, according unto thy word.

66 Teach me good judgment and knowledge; for I have believed thy commandments.

67 Before I was afflicted I went astray; but now have I kept thy word.

68 Thou art good, and doest good; teach me thy statutes.

69 The proud have forged a lie against me; but I will keep thy precepts with my whole heart.

70 Their heart is as fat as grease; but I delight in thy law.

71 It is good for me that I have been afflicted; that I might learn thy statutes.

72 The law of thy mouth is better unto me than thousands of gold and silver.

י (JOD).

73 Thy hands have made me and fashioned me; give me understanding, that I may learn thy commandments.

74 They that fear thee will be glad when they see me; because I have hoped in thy word.

75 I know, O LORD, that thy judgments are right, and that thou in faithfulness hast afflicted me.

76 Let, I pray thee, thy merciful kindness be for my comfort, according to thy word unto thy servant.

77 Let thy tender mercies come unto me, that I may live; for thy law is my delight.

78 Let the proud be ashamed; for they dealt perversely with me without a cause; but I will meditate in thy precepts.

79 Let those that fear thee turn unto me, and those that have known thy testimonies.

80 Let my heart be sound in thy statutes; that I be not ashamed.

כ (CAPH).

81 My soul fainteth for thy salvation; but I hope in thy word.

82 Mine eyes fail for thy word, saying, When wilt thou comfort me?

83 For I am become like a bottle in the smoke; yet do I not forget thy statutes.

84 How many are the days of thy servant? when wilt thou execute judgment on them that persecute me?

85 The proud have digged pits for me, which are not after thy law.

86 All thy commandments are faithful; they persecute me wrongfully; help thou me.

87 They had almost consumed me upon earth; but I forsook not thy precepts.

88 Quicken me after thy lovingkindness; so shall I keep the testimony of thy mouth.

ל (LAMED).

89 For ever, O LORD, thy word is settled in heaven.

90 Thy faithfulness is unto all generations; thou hast established the earth, and it abideth.

91 They continue this day according to thine ordinances; for all are thy servants.

92 Unless thy law had been my delights, I should then have perished in mine affliction.

93 I will never forget thy precepts; for with them thou hast quickened me.

94 I am thine, save me; for I have sought thy precepts.

95 The wicked have waited for me to destroy me; but I will consider thy testimonies.

96 I have seen an end of all perfection; but thy commandment is exceeding broad.

מ (MEM).

97 O how love I thy law! it is my meditation all the day.

98 Thou through thy commandments hast made me wiser than mine enemies; for they are ever with me.

99 I have more understanding than all my teachers; for thy testimonies are my meditation.

100 I understand more than the ancients, because I keep thy precepts.

101 I have refrained my feet from every evil way, that I might keep thy word.

102 I have not departed from thy judgments; for thou hast taught me.

103 How sweet are thy words unto my taste! yea, sweeter than honey to my mouth!

104 Through thy precepts I get understanding; therefore I hate every false way.

נ (NUN).

105 Thy word is a lamp unto my feet, and a light unto my path.

106 I have sworn, and I will perform it, that I will keep thy righteous judgments.

107 I am afflicted very much; quicken me, O LORD, according unto thy word.

108 Accept, I beseech thee, the free-will offerings of my mouth, O LORD, and teach me thy judgments.

109 My soul is continually in my hand; yet do I not forget thy law.

110 The wicked have laid a snare for me; yet I erred not from thy precepts.

111 Thy testimonies have I taken as an heritage for ever: for they are the rejoicing of my heart.

112 I have inclined my heart to perform thy statutes alway, even unto the end.

ס (SAMECH).

113 I hate vain thoughts; but thy law do I love.

114 Thou art my hiding place and my shield; I hope in thy word.

115 Depart from me, ye evildoers; for I will keep the commandments of my God.

116 Uphold me according unto thy word, that I may live; and let me not be ashamed of my hope.

117 Hold thou me up, and I shall be safe; and I will have respect unto thy statutes continually.

118 Thou hast trodden down all them that err from thy statutes; for their deceit is falsehood.

119 Thou puttest away all the wicked of the earth like dross; therefore I love thy testimonies.

120 My flesh trembleth for fear of thee; and I am afraid of thy judgments.

ע (AIN).

121 I have done judgment and justice; leave me not to mine oppressors.

122 Be surety for thy servant for good; let not the proud oppress me.

123 Mine eyes fail for thy salvation, and for the word of thy righteousness.

124 Deal with thy servant according unto thy mercy, and teach me thy statutes.

125 I am thy servant; give me understanding, that I may know thy testimonies.

126 It is time for thee, LORD, to work; for they have made void thy law.

127 Therefore I love thy commandments above gold; yea, above fine gold.

128 Therefore I esteem all thy precepts concerning all things to be right; and I hate every false way.

פ (PE).

129 Thy testimonies are wonderful; therefore doth my soul keep them.

130 The entrance of thy words giveth light; it giveth understanding unto the simple.

131 I opened my mouth, and panted; for I longed for thy commandments.

132 Look thou upon me, and be merciful unto me, as thou usest to do unto those that love thy name.

133 Order my steps in thy word; and let not any iniquity have dominion over me.

134 Deliver me from the oppression of man; so will I keep thy precepts.

135 Make thy face to shine upon thy servant; and teach me thy statutes.

136 Rivers of waters run down mine eyes, because they keep not thy law.

צ (TZADDI).

137 Righteous art thou, O LORD, and upright are thy judgments.

138 Thy testimonies that thou hast commanded are righteous and very faithful.

139 My zeal hath consumed me, because mine enemies have forgotten thy words.

140 Thy word is very pure; therefore thy servant loveth it.

141 I am small and despised; yet do not I forget thy precepts.

142 Thy righteousness is an everlasting righteousness, and thy law is the truth.

143 Trouble and anguish have taken hold on me; yet thy commandments are my delights.

144 The righteousness of thy testimonies is everlasting; give me understanding, and I shall live.

ק (Koph).

145 I cried with my whole heart; hear me, O Lord; I will keep thy statutes.

146 I cried unto thee; save me, and I shall keep thy testimonies.

147 I prevented the dawning of the morning, and cried; I hoped in thy word.

148 Mine eyes prevent the night watches, that I might meditate in thy word.

149 Hear my voice according unto thy lovingkindness; O Lord, quicken me according to thy judgment.

150 They draw nigh that follow after mischief; they are far from thy law.

151 Thou art near, O Lord; and all thy commandments are truth.

152 Concerning thy testimonies, I have known of old that thou hast founded them for ever.

ר (Resh).

153 Consider mine affliction, and deliver me; for I do not forget thy law.

154 Plead my cause, and deliver me; quicken me according to thy word.

155 Salvation is far from the wicked; for they seek not thy statutes.

156 Great are thy tender mercies, O Lord; quicken me according to thy judgments.

157 Many are my persecutors and mine enemies; yet do I not decline from thy testimonies.

158 I beheld the transgressors, and was grieved; because they kept not thy word.

159 Consider how I love thy precepts; quicken me, O Lord, according to thy lovingkindness.

160 Thy word is true from the beginning: and every one of thy righteous judgments endureth for ever.

שׁ (Schin).

161 Princes have persecuted me without a cause; but my heart standeth in awe of thy word.

162 I rejoice at thy word, as one that findeth great spoil.

163 I hate and abhor lying; but thy law do I love.

164 Seven times a day do I praise thee because of thy righteous judgments.

165 Great peace have they which love thy law; and nothing shall offend them.

166 Lord, I have hoped for thy salvation, and done thy commandments.

167 My soul hath kept thy testimonies; and I love them exceedingly.

ת (Tau).

168 I have kept thy precepts and thy testimonies; for all my ways are before thee.

169 Let my cry come near before thee, O Lord; give me understanding according to thy word.

170 Let my supplication come before thee; deliver me according to thy word.

171 My lips shall utter praise, when thou hast taught me thy statutes.

172 My tongue shall speak of thy word; for all thy commandments are righteousness.

173 Let thine hand help me; for I have chosen thy precepts.

174 I have longed for thy salvation, O Lord; and thy law is my delight.

175 Let my soul live, and it shall praise thee; and let thy judgments help me.

176 I have gone astray like a lost sheep; seek thy servant; for I do not forget thy commandments.

Psalm 139.

O LORD, thou hast searched me, and known me.
2 Thou knowest my downsitting and mine uprising; thou understandest my thought afar off.

3 Thou compassest my path and my lying down, and art acquainted with all my ways.

4 For there is not a word in my tongue, but, lo, O LORD, thou knowest it altogether.

5 Thou hast beset me behind and before, and laid thine hand upon me.

6 Such knowledge is too wonderful for me; it is high, I cannot attain unto it.

7 Whither shall I go from thy spirit? or whither shall I flee from thy presence?

8 If I ascend up into heaven, thou art there; if I make my bed in hell, behold, thou art there.

9 If I take the wings of the morning, and dwell in the uttermost parts of the sea;

10 Even there shall thy hand lead me, and thy right hand shall hold me.

11 If I say, Surely the darkness shall cover me; even the night shall be light about me.

12 Yea, the darkness hideth not from thee; but the night shineth as the day; the darkness and the light are both alike to thee.

13 For thou hast possessed my reins; thou hast covered me in my mother's womb.

14 I will praise thee; for I am fearfully and wonderfully made; marvellous are thy works; and that my soul knoweth right well.

15 My substance was not hid from thee, when I was made in secret, and curiously wrought in the lowest parts of the earth.

16 Thine eyes did see my substance, yet being unperfect; and in thy book all my members were written, which in continuance were fashioned, when as yet there was none of them.

17 How precious also are thy thoughts unto me, O God! how great is the sum of them!

18 If I should count them, they are more in number than the sand; when I awake, I am still with thee.

19 Surely thou wilt slay the wicked, O God; depart from me therefore, ye bloody men.

20 For they speak against thee wickedly, and thine enemies take thy name in vain.

21 Do not I hate them, O Lord, that hate thee? and am not I grieved with those that rise up against thee?

22 I hate them with perfect hatred; I count them mine enemies.

23 Search me, O God, and know my heart; try me, and know my thoughts;

24 And see if there be any wicked way in me, and lead me in the way everlasting.

Proverbs 2.

THE WAYS OF WISDOM.

MY son, if thou wilt receive my words, and hide my commandments with thee;

2 So that thou incline thine ear unto wisdom, and apply thine heart to understanding;

3 Yea, if thou criest after knowledge, and liftest up thy voice for understanding;

4 If thou seekest her as silver, and searchest for her as for hid treasures;

5 Then shalt thou understand the fear of the Lord, and find the knowledge of God.

6 For the Lord giveth wisdom; out of his mouth cometh knowledge and understanding.

7 He layeth up sound wisdom for the righteous; he is a buckler to them that walk uprightly.

8 He keepeth the paths of judgment, and preserveth the way of his saints.

9 Then shalt thou understand righteousness, and judgment, and equity, yea, every good path.

10 When wisdom entereth into thine heart, and knowledge is pleasant unto thy soul;

11 Discretion shall preserve thee, understanding shall keep thee;

12 To deliver thee from the way of the evil man, from the man that speaketh froward things;

13 Who leave the paths of uprightness, to walk in the ways of darkness;

14 Who rejoice to do evil, and delight in the frowardness of the wicked;

15 Whose ways are crooked, and they froward in their paths;

16 To deliver thee from the strange woman, even from the stranger which flattereth with her words;

17 Which forsaketh the guide of her youth, and forgetteth the covenant of her God.

18 For her house inclineth unto death, and her paths unto the dead.

19 None that go unto her return again, neither take they hold of the paths of life.

20 That thou mayest walk in the way of good men, and keep the paths of the righteous.

21 For the upright shall dwell in the land, and the perfect shall remain in it.

22 But the wicked shall be cut off from the earth, and the transgressors shall be rooted out of it.

Proverbs 3.

THE GAIN OF WISDOM.

MY son, forget not my law; but let thine heart keep my commandments;

2 For length of days, and long life, and peace, shall they add to thee.

3 Let not mercy and truth forsake thee; bind them about thy neck; write them upon the table of thine heart;

4 So shalt thou find favor and good understanding in the sight of God and man.

5 Trust in the LORD with all thine heart; and lean not unto thine own understanding.

6 In all thy ways acknowledge him, and he shall direct thy paths.

7 Be not wise in thine own eyes; fear the LORD, and depart from evil.

8 It shall be health to thy navel, and marrow to thy bones.

9 Honour the LORD with thy substance, and with the firstfruits of all thine increase;

10 So shall thy barns be filled with plenty, and thy presses shall burst out with new wine.

11 My son, despise not the chastening of the LORD; neither be weary of his correction;

12 For whom the LORD loveth he correcteth; even as a father the son in whom he delighteth.

13 Happy is the man that findeth wisdom, and the man that getteth understanding;

14 For the merchandise of it is better than the merchandise of silver, and the gain thereof than fine gold.

15 She is more precious than rubies; and all the things thou canst desire are not to be compared unto her.

16 Length of days is in her right hand; and in her left hand riches and honor.

17 Her ways are ways of pleasantness, and all her paths are peace.

18 She is a tree of life to them that lay hold upon her, and happy is every one that retaineth her.

19 The LORD by wisdom hath founded the earth; by understanding hath he established the heavens.

20 By his knowledge the depths are broken up, and the clouds drop down the dew.

21 My son, let not them depart from thine eyes; keep sound wisdom and discretion:

22 So shall they be life unto thy soul, and grace to thy neck.

23 Then shalt thou walk in thy way safely, and thy foot shall not stumble.

24 When thou liest down, thou shalt not be afraid; yea, thou shalt lie down, and thy sleep shall be sweet.

25 Be not afraid of sudden fear, neither of the desolation of the wicked, when it cometh.

26 For the Lord shall be thy confidence, and shall keep thy foot from being taken.

27 Withhold not good from them to whom it is due, when it is in the power of thine hand to do it.

28 Say not unto thy neighbor, Go, and come again, and to morrow I will give; when thou hast it by thee.

29 Devise not evil against thy neighbor, seeing he dwelleth securely by thee.

30 Strive not with a man without cause, if he have done thee no harm.

31 Envy thou not the oppressor, and choose none of his ways.

32 For the froward is abomination to the LORD; but his secret is with the righteous.

33 The curse of the LORD is in the house of the wicked; but he blesseth the habitation of the just.

34 Surely he scorneth the scorners; but he giveth grace unto the lowly.

35 The wise shall inherit glory; but shame shall be the promotion of fools.

Proverbs 8.

THE INVITATION OF WISDOM.

DOTH not wisdom cry? and understanding put forth her voice?

2 She standeth in the top of high places, by the way in the places of the paths.

3 She crieth at the gates, at the entry of the city, at the coming in at the doors:

4 Unto you, O men, I call; and my voice is to the sons of man.

5 O ye simple, understand wisdom; and, ye fools, be ye of an understanding heart.

6 Hear; for I will speak of excellent things; and the opening of my lips shall be right things.

7 For my mouth shall speak truth; and wickedness is an abomination to my lips.

8 All the words of my mouth are in righteousness; there is nothing froward or perverse in them.

9 They are all plain to him that understandeth, and right to them that find knowledge.

10 Receive my instruction, and not silver; and knowledge rather than choice gold.

11 For wisdom is better than rubies; and all the things that may be desired are not to be compared to it.

12 I wisdom dwell with prudence, and find out knowledge of witty inventions.

13 The fear of the LORD is to hate evil; pride, and arrogancy, and the evil way, and the froward mouth, do I hate.

14 Counsel is mine, and sound wisdom; I am understanding; I have strength.

15 By me kings reign, and princes decree justice.

16 By me princes rule, and nobles, even all the judges of the earth.

17 I love them that love me; and those that seek me early shall find me.

18 Riches and honor are with me; yea, durable riches and righteousness.

19 My fruit is better than gold, yea, than fine gold; and my revenue than choice silver.

20 I lead in the way of righteousness, in the midst of the paths of judgment;

21 That I may cause those that love me to inherit substance; and I will fill their treasures.

22 The Lord possessed me in the beginning of his way, before his works of old.

23 I was set up from everlasting, from the beginning, or ever the earth was.

24 When there were no depths, I was brought forth; when there were no fountains abounding with water.

25 Before the mountains were settled, before the hills was I brought forth;

26 While as yet he had not made the earth, nor the fields, nor the highest part of the dust of the world.

27 When he prepared the heavens, I was there; when he set a compass upon the face of the depth;

28 When he established the clouds above; when he strengthened the fountains of the deep;

29 When he gave to the sea his decree, that the waters should not pass his commandment; when he appointed the foundations of the earth;

30 Then I was by him, as one brought up with him; and I was daily his delight, rejoicing always before him;

31 Rejoicing in the habitable part of his earth; and my delights were with the sons of men.

32 Now therefore hearken unto me, O ye children; for blessed are they that keep my ways.

33 Hear instruction, and be wise, and refuse it not.

34 Blessed is the man that heareth me, watching daily at my gates, waiting at the posts of my doors.

35. For whoso findeth me findeth life, and shall obtain favor of the Lord.

36 But he that sinneth against me wrongeth his own soul; all they that hate me love death.

Proverbs 12.

THE RIGHTEOUS AND THE WICKED.

WHOSO loveth instruction loveth knowledge; but he that hateth reproof is brutish.

2 A good man obtaineth favor of the LORD; but a man of wicked devices will he condemn.

3 A man shall not be established by wickedness; but the root of the righteous shall not be moved.

4 A virtuous women is a crown to her husband; but she that maketh ashamed is as rottenness in his bones.

5 The thoughts of the righteous are right; but the counsels of the wicked are deceit.

6 The words of the wicked are to lie in wait for blood; but the mouth of the upright shall deliver them.

7 The wicked are overthrown, and are not; but the house of the righteous shall stand.

8 A man shall be commended according to his wisdom; but he that is of a perverse heart shall be despised.

9 He that is despised, and hath a servant, is better than he that honoreth himself, and lacketh bread.

10 A righteous man regardeth the life of his beast; but the tender mercies of the wicked are cruel.

11 He that tilleth his land shall be satisfied with bread; but he that followeth vain persons is void of understanding.

12 The wicked desireth the net of evil men; but the root of the righteous yieldeth fruit.

13 The wicked is snared by the transgression of his lips; but the just shall come out of trouble.

14 A man shall be satisfied with good by the fruit of his mouth; and the recompense of a man's hands shall be rendered unto him.

15 The way of a fool is right in his own eyes; but he that hearkeneth unto counsel is wise.

16 A fool's wrath is presently known; but a prudent man covereth shame.

17 He that speaketh truth showeth forth righteousness; but a false witness deceit.

18 There is that speaketh like the piercings of a sword; but the tongue of the wise is health.

19 The lip of truth shall be established for ever; but a lying tongue is but for a moment.

20 Deceit is in the heart of them that imagine evil; but to the counsellors of peace is joy.

21 There shall no evil happen to the just; but the wicked shall be filled with mischief.

22 Lying lips are abomination to the LORD; but they that deal truly are his delight.

23 A prudent man concealeth knowledge; but the heart of fools proclaimeth foolishness.

24 The hand of the diligent shall bear rule; but the slothful shall be under tribute.

25 Heaviness in the heart of man maketh it stoop; but a good word maketh it glad.

26 The righteous is more excellent than his neighbor; but the way of the wicked seduceth them.

27 The slothful man roasteth not that which he took in hunting; but the substance of a diligent man is precious.

28 In the way of righteousness is life; and in the pathway thereof there is no death.

Isaiah 58.

TRUE AND FALSE RELIGION.

CRY aloud, spare not, lift up thy voice like a trumpet, and show my people their transgression, and the house of Jacob their sins.

2 Yet they seek me daily, and delight to know my ways, as a nation that did righteousness, and forsook not the ordinance of their God; they ask of me the ordinances of justice; they take delight in approaching to God.

3 Wherefore have we fasted, say they, and thou seest not? wherefore have we afflicted our soul, and thou takest no knowledge? Behold, in the day of your fast ye find pleasure, and exact all your labors.

4 Behold, ye fast for strife and debate, and to smite with the fist of wickedness; ye shall not fast as ye do this day, to make your voice to be heard on high.

5 Is it such a fast that I have chosen? a day for a man to afflict his soul? is it to bow down his head as a bulrush, and to spread sackcloth and ashes under him? wilt thou call this a fast, and an acceptable day to the LORD?

6 Is not this the fast that I have chosen? to loose the bands of wickedness, to undo the heavy burdens, and to let the oppressed go free, and that ye break every yoke?

7 Is it not to deal thy bread to the hungry, and that thou bring the poor that are cast out to thy house? when thou seest the naked, that thou cover him? and that thou hide not thyself from thine own flesh?

8 Then shall thy light break forth as the morning, and thine health shall spring forth speedily, and thy righteousness shall go before thee; the glory of the LORD shall be thy rearward.

9 Then shalt thou call, and the LORD shall answer; thou shalt cry, and he shall say, Here I am. If thou take away from the midst of thee the yoke, the putting forth of the finger, and speaking vanity;

10 And if thou draw out thy soul to the hungry, and satisfy the afflicted soul; then shall thy light rise in obscurity, and thy darkness be as the noon day;

11 And the LORD shall guide thee continually, and satisfy thy soul in drought, and make fat thy bones; and thou shalt be like a watered garden, and like a spring of water, whose waters fail not.

12 And they that shall be of thee shall build the old waste places; thou shalt raise up the foundations of many generations; and thou shalt be called, The repairer of the breach, The restorer of paths to dwell in.

13 If thou turn away thy foot from the sabbath, from doing thy

pleasure on my holy day; and call the sabbath a delight, the holy of the LORD, honorable; and shalt honor him, not doing thine own ways, nor finding thine own pleasure, nor speaking thine own words;

14 Then shalt thou delight thyself in the LORD, and I will cause thee to ride upon the high places of the earth, and feed thee with the heritage of Jacob thy father; for the mouth of the LORD hath spoken it.

Matthew 5.

THE SERMON ON THE MOUNT.

AND seeing the multitudes, he went up into a mountain; and when he was set, his disciples came unto him;

2 And he opened his mouth, and taught them, saying,

3 Blessed are the poor in spirit, for theirs is the kingdom of heaven.

4 Blessed are they that mourn, for they shall be comforted.

5 Blessed are the meek, for they shall inherit the earth.

6 Blessed are they which do hunger and thirst after righteousness, for they shall be filled.

7 Blessed are the merciful, for they shall obtain mercy.

8 Blessed are the pure in heart, for they shall see God.

9 Blessed are the peacemakers, for they shall be called the children of God.

10 Blessed are they which are persecuted for righteousness' sake, for theirs is the kingdom of heaven.

11 Blessed are ye, when men shall revile you, and persecute you, and shall say all manner of evil against you falsely, for my sake.

12 Rejoice, and be exceeding glad, for great is your reward in heaven; for so persecuted they the prophets which were before you.

13 Ye are the salt of the earth; but if the salt have lost his

savor, wherewith shall it be salted? it is thenceforth good for nothing, but to be cast out, and to be trodden under foot of men.

14 Ye are the light of the world. A city that is set on an hill cannot be hid.

15 Neither do men light a candle, and put it under a bushel, but on a candlestick; and it giveth light unto all that are in the house.

16 Let your light so shine before men, that they may see your good works, and glorify your Father which is in heaven.

17 Think not that I am come to destroy the law, or the prophets; I am not come to destroy, but to fulfil.

18 For verily I say unto you, Till heaven and earth pass, one jot or one tittle shall in no wise pass from the law, till all be fulfilled.

19 Whosoever therefore shall break one of these least commandments, and shall teach men so, he shall be called the least in the kingdom of heaven; but whosoever shall do and teach them, the same shall be called great in the kingdom of heaven.

20 For I say unto you, That except your righteousness shall exceed the righteousness of the scribes and Pharisees, ye shall in no case enter into the kingdom of heaven.

21 Ye have heard that it was said by them of old time, Thou shalt not kill, and whosoever shall kill shall be in danger of the judgment;

22 But I say unto you, That whosoever is angry with his brother without a cause shall be in danger of the judgment, and whosoever shall say to his brother, Raca, shall be in danger of the council; but whosoever shall say, Thou fool, shall be in danger of hell fire.

23 Therefore if thou bring thy gift to the altar, and there rememberest that thy brother hath aught against thee,

24 Leave there thy gift before the altar, and go thy way; first be reconciled to thy brother, and then come and offer thy gift.

25 Agree with thine adversary quickly, while thou art in the way with him; lest at any time the adversary deliver thee to the judge, and the judge deliver thee to the officer, and thou be cast into prison.

26 Verily I say unto thee, Thou shalt by no means come out thence, till thou hast paid the uttermost farthing.

27 Ye have heard that it was said by them of old time, Thou shalt not commit adultery;

28 But I say unto you, That whosoever looketh on a woman to lust after her hath committed adultery with her already in his heart.

29 And if thy right eye offend thee, pluck it out, and cast it from thee; for it is profitable for thee that one of thy members should perish, and not that thy whole body should be cast into hell.

30 And if thy right hand offend thee, cut it off, and cast it from thee; for it is profitable for thee that one of thy members should perish, and not that thy whole body should be cast into hell.

31 It hath been said, Whosoever shall put away his wife, let him give her a writing of divorcement:

32 But I say unto you, That whosoever shall put away his wife, saving for the cause of fornication, causeth her to commit adultery; and whosoever shall marry her that is divorced committeth adultery.

33 Again, ye have heard that it hath been said by them of old time, Thou shalt not forswear thyself, but shalt perform unto the Lord thine oaths;

34 But I say unto you, Swear not at all; neither by heaven, for it is God's throne;

35 Nor by the earth, for it is his footstool; neither by Jerusalem, for it is the city of the great King.

36 Neither shalt thou swear by thy head, because thou canst not make one hair white or black.

37 But let your communication be, Yea, yea; Nay, nay; for whatsoever is more than these cometh of evil.

38 Ye have heard that it hath been said, An eye for an eye, and a tooth for a tooth;

39 But I say unto you, That ye resist not evil; but whosoever shall smite thee on thy right cheek, turn to him the other also.

40 And if any man will sue thee at the law, and take away thy coat, let him have thy cloak also.

41 And whosoever shall compel thee to go a mile, go with him twain.

42 Give to him that asketh thee, and from him that would borrow of thee turn not thou away.

43 Ye have heard that it hath been said, Thou shalt love thy neighbor, and hate thine enemy.

44 But I say unto you, Love your enemies, bless them that curse you, do good to them that hate you, and pray for them which despitefully use you and persecute you;

45 That ye may be the children of your Father which is in heaven; for he maketh his sun to rise on the evil and on the good, and sendeth rain on the just and on the unjust.

46 For if ye love them which love you, what reward have ye? do not even the publicans the same?

47 And if ye salute your brethren only, what do ye more than others? do not even the publicans so?

48 Be ye therefore perfect, even as your Father which is in heaven is perfect.

Matthew 6.

THE SERMON ON THE MOUNT.

TAKE heed that ye do not your alms before men, to be seen of them; otherwise ye have no reward of your Father which is in heaven.

2 Therefore when thou doest thine alms, do not sound a trumpet before thee, as the hypocrites do in the synagogues and in the streets, that they may have glory of men. Verily I say unto you, They have their reward.

3 But when thou doest alms, let not thy left hand know what thy right hand doeth,

4 That thine alms may be in secret; and thy Father which seeth in secret himself shall reward thee openly.

5 And when thou prayest, thou shalt not be as the hypocrites

are; for they love to pray standing in the synagogues and in the corners of the streets, that they may be seen of men. Verily I say unto you, They have their reward.

6 But thou, when thou prayest, enter into thy closet, and when thou hast shut thy door, pray to thy Father which is in secret; and thy Father which seeth in secret shall reward thee openly.

7 But when ye pray use not vain repetitions, as the heathen do; for they think that they shall be heard for their much speaking.

8 Be not ye therefore like unto them; for your Father knoweth what things ye have need of, before ye ask him.

9 After this manner therefore pray ye: Our Father which art in heaven, Hallowed be thy name.

10 Thy kingdom come. Thy will be done in earth, as it is in heaven.

11 Give us this day our daily bread.

12 And forgive us our debts, as we forgive our debtors.

13 And lead us not into temptation, but deliver us from evil; For thine is the kingdom, and the power, and the glory, for ever. Amen.

14. For if ye forgive men their trespasses, your heavenly Father will also forgive you;

15 But if ye forgive not men their trespasses, neither will your Father forgive your trespasses.

16 Moreover when ye fast, be not, as the hypocrites, of a sad countenance; for they disfigure their faces, that they may appear unto men to fast. Verily I say unto you, They have their reward.

17 But thou, when thou fastest, anoint thine head, and wash thy face;

18 That thou appear not unto men to fast, but unto thy Father which is in secret; and thy Father, which seeth in secret, shall reward thee openly.

19 Lay not up for yourselves treasures upon earth, where moth and rust doth corrupt, and where thieves break through and steal;

20 But lay up for yourselves treasures in heaven, where neither moth nor rust doth corrupt, and where thieves do not break through nor steal;

21 For where your treasure is, there will your heart be also.

22 The light of the body is the eye; if therefore thine eye be single, thy whole body shall be full of light.

23 But if thine eye be evil, thy whole body shall be full of darkness. If therefore the light that is in thee be darkness, how great is that darkness!

24 No man can serve two masters; for either he will hate the one, and love the other, or else he will hold to the one, and despise the other. Ye cannot serve God and mammon.

25 Therefore I say unto you, Take no thought for your life, what ye shall eat, or what ye shall drink; nor yet for your body, what ye shall put on. Is not the life more than meat, and the body than raiment?

26 Behold the fowls of the air, for they sow not, neither do they reap nor gather into barns; yet your heavenly Father feedeth them. Are ye not much better than they?

27 Which of you by taking thought can add one cubit unto his stature?

28 And why take ye thought for raiment? Consider the lilies of the field, how they grow; they toil not, neither do they spin;

29 And yet I say unto you, That even Solomon in all his glory was not arrayed like one of these.

30 Wherefore if God so clothe the grass of the field, which to day is, and to morrow is cast into the oven, shall he not much more clothe you, O ye of little faith?

31 Therefore take no thought, saying, What shall we eat? or, What shall we drink? or, Wherewithal shall we be clothed?

32 (For after all these things do the Gentiles seek;) for your heavenly Father knoweth that ye have need of all these things.

33 But seek ye first the kingdom of God, and his righteousness; and all these things shall be added unto you.

34 Take therefore no thought for the morrow, for the morrow shall take thought for the things of itself. Sufficient unto the day is the evil thereof.

Matthew 7.

THE SERMON ON THE MOUNT.

JUDGE not, that ye be not judged.

2 For with what judgment ye judge, ye shall be judged; and with what measure ye mete, it shall be measured to you again.

3 And why beholdest thou the mote that is in thy brother's eye, but considerest not the beam that is in thine own eye?

4 Or how wilt thou say to thy brother, Let me pull out the mote out of thine eye; and behold, a beam is in thine own eye?

5 Thou hypocrite, first cast out the beam out of thine own eye, and then shalt thou see clearly to cast out the mote out of thy brother's eye.

6 Give not that which is holy unto the dogs, neither cast ye your pearls before swine, lest they trample them under their feet, and turn again and rend you.

7 Ask, and it shall be given you; seek, and ye shall find; knock, and it shall be opened unto you;

8 For every one that asketh receiveth; and he that seeketh findeth; and to him that knocketh it shall be opened.

9 Or what man is there of you, whom if his son ask bread, will he give him a stone?

10 Or if he ask a fish, will he give him a serpent?

11 If ye then, being evil, know how to give good gifts unto your children, how much more shall your Father which is in heaven give good things to them that ask him?

12 Therefore all things whatsoever ye would that men should do to you, do ye even so to them; for this is the law and the prophets.

13 Enter ye in at the strait gate; for wide is the gate, and broad is the way, that leadeth to destruction, and many there be which go in thereat;

14 Because strait is the gate, and narrow is the way, which leadeth unto life, and few there be that find it.

15 Beware of false prophets, which come to you in sheep's clothing, but inwardly they are ravening wolves.

16 Ye shall know them by their fruits. Do men gather grapes of thorns, or figs of thistles?

17 Even so every good tree bringeth forth good fruit; but a corrupt tree bringeth forth evil fruit.

18 A good tree cannot bring forth evil fruit, neither can a corrupt tree bring forth good fruit.

19 Every tree that bringeth not forth good fruit is hewn down, and cast into the fire.

20 Wherefore by their fruits ye shall know them.

21 Not every one that saith unto me, Lord, Lord, shall enter into the kingdom of heaven; but he that doeth the will of my Father which is in heaven.

22 Many will say to me in that day, Lord, Lord, have we not prophesied in thy name, and in thy name have cast out devils, and in thy name done many wonderful works?

23 And then will I profess unto them, I never knew you; depart from me, ye that work iniquity.

24 Therefore whosoever heareth these sayings of mine, and doeth them, I will liken him unto a wise man, which built his house upon a rock;

25 And the rain descended, and the floods came, and the winds blew, and beat upon that house; and it fell not; for it was founded upon a rock.

26 And every one that heareth these sayings of mine, and doeth them not, shall be likened unto a foolish man, which built his house upon the sand;

27 And the rain descended, and the floods came, and the winds blew, and beat upon that house; and it fell; and great was the fall of it.

28 And it came to pass, when Jesus had ended these sayings, the people were astonished at his doctrine;

29 For he taught them as one having authority, and not as the scribes.

The Acts 26.

PAUL BEFORE AGRIPPA.

THEN Agrippa said unto Paul, Thou art permitted to speak for thyself. Then Paul stretched forth the hand, and answered for himself:

2 I think myself happy, king Agrippa, because I shall answer for myself this day before thee touching all the things whereof I am accused of the Jews,

3 Especially because I know thee to be expert in all customs and questions which are among the Jews; wherefore I beseech thee to hear me patiently.

4 My manner of life from my youth, which was at the first among mine own nation at Jerusalem, know all the Jews;

5 Which knew me from the beginning, if they would testify, that after the most straitest sect of our religion I lived a Pharisee.

6 And now I stand and am judged for the hope of the promise made of God unto our fathers;

7 Unto which promise our twelve tribes, instantly serving God day and night, hope to come. For which hope's sake, king Agrippa, I am accused of the Jews.

8 Why should it be thought a thing incredible with you, that God should raise the dead?

9 I verily thought with myself that I ought to do many things contrary to the name of Jesus of Nazareth.

10 Which thing I also did in Jerusalem; and many of the saints did I shut up in prison, having received authority from the chief priests; and when they were put to death, I gave my voice against them.

11 And I punished them oft in every synagogue, and compelled them to blaspheme; and being exceedingly mad against them, I persecuted them even unto strange cities.

12 Whereupon as I went to Damascus with authority and commission from the chief priests,

13 At midday, O king, I saw in the way a light from heaven, above the brightness of the sun, shining round about me and them which journeyed with me.

14 And when we were all fallen to the earth, I heard a voice speaking unto me, and saying in the Hebrew tongue, Saul, Saul, why persecutest thou me? it is hard for thee to kick against the pricks.

15 And I said, Who art thou, Lord? And he said, I am Jesus whom thou persecutest.

16 But rise, and stand upon thy feet; for I have appeared unto thee for this purpose, to make thee a minister and a witness both of these things which thou hast seen, and of those things in the which I will appear unto thee;

17 Delivering thee from the people, and from the Gentiles, unto whom now I send thee,

18 To open their eyes, and to turn them from darkness to light, and from the power of Satan unto God, that they may receive forgiveness of sins, and inheritance among them which are sanctified by faith that is in me.

19 Whereupon, O king Agrippa, I was not disobedient unto the heavenly vision:

20 But showed first unto them of Damascus, and at Jerusalem, and throughout all the coasts of Judea, and then to the Gentiles, that they should repent and turn to God, and do works meet for repentance.

21 For these causes the Jews caught me in the temple, and went about to kill me.

22 Having therefore obtained help of God, I continue unto this day, witnessing both to small and great, saying none other things than those which the prophets and Moses did say should come:

23 That Christ should suffer, and that he should be the first that should rise from the dead, and should show light unto the people, and to the Gentiles.

24 And as he thus spake for himself, Festus said with a loud voice, Paul, thou art beside thyself; much learning doth make thee mad.

25 But he said, I am not mad, most noble Festus, but speak forth the words of truth and soberness.

26 For the king knoweth of these things, before whom also I speak freely; for I am persuaded that none of these things are hidden from him; for this thing was not done in a corner.

27 King Agrippa, believest thou the prophets? I know that thou believest.

28 Then Agrippa said unto Paul, Almost thou persuadest me to be a Christian.

29 And Paul said, I would to God that not only thou, but also all that hear me this day, were both almost, and altogether such as I am, except these bonds.

30 And when he had thus spoken, the king rose up, and the governor, and Bernice, and they that sat with them;

31 And when they were gone aside, they talked between themselves, saying, This man doeth nothing worthy of death or of bonds.

32 Then said Agrippa unto Festus, This man might have been set at liberty, if he had not appealed unto Cæsar.

1 Corinthians 13.

LOVE BEYOND ALL THINGS.

THOUGH I speak with the tongues of men and of angels, and have not charity, I am become as sounding brass, or a tinkling cymbal.

2 And though I have the gift of prophecy, and understand all mysteries, and all knowledge; and though I have all faith, so that I could remove mountains, and have not charity, I am nothing.

3 And though I bestow all my goods to feed the poor, and though I give my body to be burned, and have not charity, it profiteth me nothing.

4 Charity suffereth long, and is kind; charity envieth not; charity vaunteth not itself, is not puffed up,

5 Doth not behave itself unseemly, seeketh not her own, is not easily provoked, thinketh no evil;

6 Rejoiceth not in iniquity, but rejoiceth in the truth;

7 Beareth all things, believeth all things, hopeth all things, endureth all things.

8 Charity never faileth; but whether there be prophecies, they shall fail; whether there be tongues, they shall cease; whether there be knowledge, it shall vanish away.

9 For we know in part, and we prophesy in part.

10 But when that which is perfect is come, then that which is in part shall be done away.

11 When I was a child, I spake as a child, I understood as a child, I thought as a child; but when I became a man, I put away childish things.

12 For now we see through a glass, darkly, but then face to face; now I know in part, but then shall I know even as also I am known.

13 And now abideth faith, hope, charity, these three; but the greatest of these is charity.

---

1 Corinthians 15.

THE RESURRECTION FROM THE DEAD.

MOREOVER, brethren, I declare unto you the gospel which I preached unto you, which also ye have received, and wherein ye stand;

2 By which also ye are saved, if ye keep in memory what I preached unto you, unless ye have believed in vain.

3 For I delivered unto you first of all that which I also received, how that Christ died for our sins according to the scriptures,

4 And that he was buried, and that he rose again the third day according to the scriptures,

5 And that he was seen of Cephas, then of the twelve;

6 After that, he was seen of above five hundred brethren at

once, of whom the greater part remain unto this present, but some are fallen asleep;

7 After that, he was seen of James; then of all the apostles;

8 And last of all he was seen of me also, as of one born out of due time.

9 For I am the least of the apostles, that am not meet to be called an apostle, because I persecuted the church of God.

10 But by the grace of God I am what I am; and his grace which was bestowed upon me was not in vain; but I labored more abundantly than they all; yet not I, but the grace of God which was with me.

11 Therefore whether it were I or they, so we preached, and so ye believed.

12 Now if Christ be preached that he rose from the dead, how say some among you that there is no resurrection of the dead?

13 But if there be no resurrection of the dead, then is Christ not risen;

14 And if Christ be not risen, then is our preaching vain, and your faith is also vain.

15 Yea, and we are found false witnesses of God, because we have testified of God that he raised up Christ; whom he raised not up, if so be that the dead rise not.

16 For if the dead rise not, then is not Christ raised;

17 And if Christ be not raised, your faith is vain; ye are yet in your sins.

18 Then they also which are fallen asleep in Christ are perished.

19 If in this life only we have hope in Christ, we are of all men most miserable.

20 But now is Christ risen from the dead, and become the firstfruits of them that slept.

21 For since by man came death, by man came also the resurrection of the dead.

22 For as in Adam all die, even so in Christ shall all be made alive.

23 But every man in his own order; Christ the firstfruits, afterward they that are Christ's at his coming.

24 Then cometh the end, when he shall have delivered up the kingdom to God, even the Father; when he shall have put down all rule and all authority and power.

25 For he must reign till he hath put all enemies under his feet.

26 The last enemy that shall be destroyed is death.

27 For he hath put all things under his feet. But when he saith all things are put under him, it is manifest that he is excepted, which did put all things under him.

28 And when all things shall be subdued unto him, then shall the Son also himself be subject unto him that put all things under him, that God may be all in all.

29 Else what shall they do which are baptized for the dead, if the dead rise not at all? why are they then baptized for the dead?

30 And why stand we in jeopardy every hour?

31 I protest by your rejoicing which I have in Christ Jesus our Lord, I die daily.

32 If after the manner of men I have fought with beasts at Ephesus, what advantageth it me, if the dead rise not? let us eat and drink, for to morrow we die.

33 Be not deceived; evil communications corrupt good manners.

34 Awake to righteousness, and sin not; for some have not the knowledge of God; I speak this to your shame.

35 But some man will say, How are the dead raised up? and with what body do they come?

36 Thou fool, that which thou sowest is not quickened, except it die;

37 And that which thou sowest, thou sowest not that body that shall be, but bare grain, it may chance of wheat, or of some other grain;

38 But God giveth it a body as it hath pleased him, and to every seed his own body.

39 All flesh is not the same flesh; but there is one kind of flesh of men, another flesh of beasts, another of fishes, and another of birds.

40 There are also celestial bodies, and bodies terrestrial; but the glory of the celestial is one, and the glory of the terrestrial is another.

41 There is one glory of the sun, and another glory of the moon, and another glory of the stars; for one star differeth from another star in glory.

42 So also is the resurrection of the dead. It is sown in corruption, it is raised in incorruption;

43 It is sown in dishonor, it is raised in glory; it is sown in weakness, it is raised in power;

44 It is sown a natural body, it is raised a spiritual body. There is a natural body, and there is a spiritual body.

45 And so it is written, The first man Adam was made a living soul; the last Adam was made a quickening spirit.

46 Howbeit that was not first which is spiritual, but that which is natural; and afterward that which is spiritual.

47 The first man is of the earth, earthy; the second man is the Lord from heaven.

48 As is the earthy, such are they also that are earthy; and as is the heavenly, such are they also that are heavenly.

49 And as we have borne the image of the earthy, we shall also bear the image of the heavenly.

50 Now this I say, brethren, that flesh and blood cannot inherit the kingdom of God; neither doth corruption inherit incorruption.

51 Behold, I show you a mystery; We shall not all sleep, but we shall all be changed,

52 In a moment, in the twinkling of an eye, at the last trump; for the trumpet shall sound, and the dead shall be raised incorruptible, and we shall be changed.

53 For this corruptible must put on incorruption, and this mortal must put on immortality.

54 So when this corruptible shall have put on incorruption, and this mortal shall have put on immortality, then shall be brought to pass the saying that is written, Death is swallowed up in victory.

55 O death, where is thy sting? O grave, where is thy victory?

56 The sting of death is sin; and the strength of sin is the law.

57 But thanks be to God, which giveth us the victory through our Lord Jesus Christ.

58 Therefore, my beloved brethren, be ye stedfast, unmoveable, always abounding in the work of the Lord, forasmuch as ye know that your labor is not in vain in the Lord.

James 4.

SUNDRY PRECEPTS.

FROM whence come wars and fightings among you? come they not hence, even of your lusts that war in your members?

2 Ye lust, and have not; ye kill, and desire to have, and cannot obtain; ye fight and war, yet ye have not, because ye ask not.

3 Ye ask, and receive not, because ye ask amiss, that ye may consume it upon your lusts.

4 Ye adulterers and adulteresses, know ye not that the friendship of the world is enmity with God? whosoever therefore will be a friend of the world is the enemy of God.

5 Do ye think that the scripture saith in vain, The spirit that dwelleth in us lusteth to envy?

6 But he giveth more grace. Wherefore he saith, God resisteth the proud, but giveth grace unto the humble.

7 Submit yourselves, therefore, to God. Resist the devil, and he will flee from you.

8 Draw nigh to God and he will draw nigh to you. Cleanse your hands, ye sinners; and purify your hearts, ye double minded.

9 Be afflicted, and mourn and weep; let your laughter be turned to mourning, and your joy to heaviness.

10 Humble yourself in the sight of the Lord, and he shall lift you up.

11 Speak not evil one of another, brethren. He that speaketh evil of his brother, and judgeth his brother, speaketh evil of the law, and judgeth the law; but if thou judge the law, thou art not a doer of the law, but a judge.

12 There is one lawgiver, who is able to save and to destroy: who art thou that judgest another?

13 Go to now, ye that say, To day or to morrow we will go into such a city, and continue there a year, and buy and sell, and get gain;

14 Whereas ye know not what shall be on the morrow. For what is your life? It is even a vapor, that appeareth for a little time, and then vanisheth away.

15 For that ye ought to say, If the Lord will, we shall live, and do this, or that.

16 But now ye rejoice in your boastings; all such rejoicing is evil.

17 Therefore to him that knoweth to do good, and doeth it not, to him it is sin.

Revelation 5.

THE NEW SONG.

AND I saw in the right hand of him that sat on the throne a book written within and on the backside, sealed with seven seals.

2 And I saw a strong angel proclaiming with a loud voice, Who is worthy to open the book, and to loose the seals thereof!

3 And no man in heaven, nor in earth, neither under the earth, was able to open the book, neither to look thereon.

4 And I wept much, because no man was found worthy to open and to read the book, neither to look thereon.

5 And one of the elders saith unto me, Weep not; behold, the

Lion of the tribe of Juda, the Root of David, hath prevailed to open the book, and to loose the seven seals thereof.

6 And I beheld, and lo, in the midst of the throne and of the four beasts, and in the midst of the elders, stood a Lamb as it had been slain, having seven horns and seven eyes, which are the seven Spirits of God sent forth into all the earth.

7 And he came and took the book out of the right hand of him that sat upon the throne.

8 And when he had taken the book, the four beasts and four and twenty elders fell down before the Lamb, having every one of them harps, and golden vials full of odors, which are the prayers of saints.

9 And they sung a new song, saying, Thou art worthy to take the book, and to open the seals thereof; for thou wast slain, and hast redeemed us to God by thy blood out of every kindred, and tongue, and people, and nation;

10 And hast made us unto our God kings and priests; and we shall reign on the earth.

11 And I beheld, and I heard the voice of many angels round about the throne and the beasts and the elders; and the number of them was ten thousand times ten thousand, and thousands of thousands;

12 Saying with a loud voice, Worthy is the Lamb that was slain to receive power, and riches, and wisdom, and strength, and honor, and glory, and blessing.

13 And every creature which is in heaven, and on the earth, and under the earth, and such as are in the sea, and all that are in them, heard I saying, Blessing, and honor, and glory, and power, be unto him that sitteth upon the throne, and unto the Lamb for ever and ever.

14 And the four beasts said, Amen. And the four and twenty elders fell down and worshipped him that liveth for ever and ever.

Revelation 6.

THE SEVEN SEALS.

AND I saw when the Lamb opened one of the seals, and I heard, as it were the noise of thunder, one of the four beasts saying, Come and see.

2 And I saw, and behold a white horse; and he that sat on him had a bow; and a crown was given unto him; and he went forth conquering, and to conquer.

3 And when he had opened the second seal, I heard the second beast say, Come and see.

4 And there went out another horse that was red; and power was given to him that sat thereon to take peace from the earth, and that they should kill one another; and there was given unto him a great sword.

5 And when he had opened the third seal, I heard the third beast say, Come and see. And I beheld, and lo a black horse; and he that sat on him had a pair of balances in his hand.

6 And I heard a voice in the midst of the four beasts say, A measure of wheat for a penny, and three measures of barley for a penny; and see thou hurt not the oil and the wine.

7 And when he had opened the fourth seal, I heard the voice of the fourth beast say, Come and see.

8 And I looked, and behold a pale horse; and his name that sat on him was death, and Hell followed with him. And power was given unto them over the fourth part of the earth, to kill with sword, and with hunger, and with death, and with the beasts of the earth.

9 And when he had opened the fifth seal, I saw under the altar the souls of them that were slain for the word of God, and for the testimony which they held;

10 And they cried with a loud voice, saying, How long, O LORD, holy and true, dost thou not judge and avenge our blood on them that dwell on the earth?

11 And white robes were given unto every one of them; and it was said unto them, that they should rest yet for a little season, until their fellowservants also and their brethren, that should be killed as they were, should be fulfilled.

12 And I beheld when he had opened the sixth seal, and lo, there was a great earthquake; and the sun became black as sackcloth of hair, and the moon became as blood;

13 And the stars of heaven fell unto the earth, even as a fig tree casteth her untimely figs, when she is shaken of a mighty wind.

14 And the heaven departed as a scroll when it is rolled together; and every mountain and island were moved out of their places.

15 And when the kings of the earth, and the great men, and the rich men, and the chief captains, and the mighty men, and every bondman, and every free man, hid themselves in the dens and in the rocks of the mountains;

16 And said to the mountains and rocks, Fall on us, and hide us from the face of him that sitteth on the throne, and from the wrath of the Lamb;

17 For the great day of his wrath is come, and who shall be able to stand?

www.ingramcontent.com/pod-product-compliance
Lightning Source LLC
Chambersburg PA
CBHW031600170426
43196CB00032B/712